W9-BGZ-231

I/O Consolidation in the Data Center

A Complete Guide to Data Center Ethernet and Fibre Channel over Ethernet

Silvano Gai

Claudio DeSanti

Cisco Press

800 East 96th Street

Indianapolis, Indiana 46240 USA

I/O Consolidation in the Data Center

A Complete Guide to Data Center Ethernet and Fibre Channel over Ethernet

Silvano Gai, Claudio DeSanti

Copyright© 2010 Cisco Systems, Inc.

Published by:

Cisco Press

800 East 96th Street

Indianapolis, IN 46240 USA

All rights reserved. No part of this book may be reproduced or transmitted in any form or by any means, electronic or mechanical, including photocopying, recording, or by any information storage and retrieval system, without written permission from the publisher, except for the inclusion of brief quotations in a review.

Printed in the United States of America 1 2 3 4 5 6 7 8 9 0

First Printing September 2009

Library of Congress Cataloging-in-Publication Data is available upon request.

ISBN-13: 978-1-58705-888-2

ISBN-10: 1-58705-888-X

Warning and Disclaimer

This book is designed to provide information about Data Center Ethernet and Fibre Channel over Ethernet. Every effort has been made to make this book as complete and as accurate as possible, but no warranty or fitness is implied.

The information is provided on an "as is" basis. The authors, Cisco Press, and Cisco Systems, Inc., shall have neither liability nor responsibility to any person or entity with respect to any loss or damages arising from the information contained in this book or from the use of the discs or programs that may accompany it.

The opinions expressed in this book belong to the author and are not necessarily those of Cisco Systems, Inc.

Feedback Information

At Cisco Press, our goal is to create in-depth technical books of the highest quality and value. Each book is crafted with care and precision, undergoing rigorous development that involves the unique expertise of members from the professional technical community.

Readers' feedback is a natural continuation of this process. If you have any comments regarding how we could improve the quality of this book, or otherwise alter it to better suit your needs, you can contact us through e-mail at feedback@ciscopress.com. Please make sure to include the book title and ISBN in your message.

We greatly appreciate your assistance.

Corporate and Government Sales

Cisco Press offers excellent discounts on this book when ordered in quantity for bulk purchases or special sales. For more information, please contact: U.S. Corporate and Government Sales 1-800-382-3419 corpsales@pearsontechgroup.com

For sales outside of the U.S. please contact: International Sales

international@pearsoned.com

Trademark Acknowledgments

All terms mentioned in this book that are known to be trademarks or service marks have been appropriately capitalized. Cisco Press or Cisco Systems, Inc. cannot attest to the accuracy of this information. Use of a term in this book should not be regarded as affecting the validity of any trademark or service mark.

Publisher: Paul Boger

Associate Publisher: Dave Dusthimer

Manager Global Certification: Erik Ullanderson

Business Operation Manager, Cisco Press: Anand Sundaram

Executive Editor: Mary Beth Ray

Managing Editor: Patrick Kanouse

Project Editor: Bethany Wall

Compositor: Macmillan Publishing Solutions

Proofreader: Apostrophe Editing Services

ı|ı.ı|ı.
CISCO.

Americas Headquarters
Cisco Systems, Inc.
San Jose, CA

Asia Pacific Headquarters
Cisco Systems (USA) Pte. Ltd.
Singapore

Europe Headquarters
Cisco Systems International BV
Amsterdam, The Netherlands

Cisco has more than 200 offices worldwide. Addresses, phone numbers, and fax numbers are listed on the Cisco Website at www.cisco.com/go/offices.

CCDE, CCENT, Cisco Eos, Cisco HealthPresence, the Cisco logo, Cisco Lumin, Cisco Nexus, Cisco StadiumVision, Cisco TelePresence, Cisco WebEx, DCE, and Welcome to the Human Network are trademarks; Changing the Way We Work, Live, Play, and Learn and Cisco Store are service marks; and Access Registrar, Aironet, AsyncOS, Bringing the Meeting To You, Catalyst, CCDA, CCDP, CCIE, CCIP, CCNA, CCNP, CCSP, CCVP, Cisco, the Cisco Certified Internetwork Expert logo, Cisco IOS, Cisco Press, Cisco Systems, Cisco Systems Capital, the Cisco Systems logo, Cisco Unity, Collaboration Without Limitation, EtherFast, EtherSwitch, Event Center, Fast Step, Follow Me Browsing, FormShare, GigaDrive, HomeLink, Internet Quotient, IOS, iPhone, iQuick Study, IronPort, the IronPort logo, LightStream, Linksys, MediaTone, MeetingPlace, MeetingPlace Chime Sound, MGX, Networkers, Networking Academy, Network Registrar, PCNow, PIX, PowerPanels, ProConnect, ScriptShare, SenderBase, SMARTnet, Spectrum Expert, StackWise, The Fastest Way to Increase Your Internet Quotient, TransPath, WebEx, and the WebEx logo are registered trademarks of Cisco Systems, Inc. and/or its affiliates in the United States and certain other countries.

All other trademarks mentioned in this document or website are the property of their respective owners. The use of the word partner does not imply a partnership relationship between Cisco and any other company. (0812R)

About the Authors: Silvano Gai

Silvano Gai, who grew up in a small village near Asti, Italy, has more than 27 years of experience in computer engineering and computer networks. He is the author of several books and technical publications on computer networking and multiple Internet Drafts and RFCs. He is responsible for 30 issued patents and 50 patent applications. His background includes 7 years as a full professor of computer engineering, tenure track, at Politecnico di Torino, Italy, and seven years as a researcher at the CNR (Italian National Council for Scientific Research). For the past 12 years, he has been in Silicon Valley where, in the position of Cisco Fellow, he was an architect of the Cisco Catalyst family of network switches, of the Cisco MDS family of storage networking switches, and of the Nexus family of data center switches. Silvano teaches a course on I/O Consolidation, Data Center Ethernet, and Fibre Channel over Ethernet at Stanford University (see http://scpd.stanford.edu/certificates/fcoe).

About the Authors: Claudio DeSanti

Claudio DeSanti is a Distinguished Engineer in the Advanced Architectures & Research organization at Cisco. He represents Cisco in several National and International Standards Bodies, such as INCITS Technical Committee T11, IEEE 802.1, IETF, and in industry associations. He is vice chairman of the INCITS T11 Technical Committee, chairperson of various working groups, including FC-BB-5, where FCoE has been developed, and technical editor of different standards, including IEEE 802.1Qbb, where Priority-based Flow Control is defined. He is author of several patents and international publications, including ten RFCs in IETF and other standards in the American National Standard Institute. He received many honors and awards, including the INCITS 2008 Technical Excellence Award, the INCITS 2007 Team Award, and the INCITS 2006 Gene Milligan Award for Effective Committee Management. Claudio's research interests include network protocols, storage networking, routing, and security. He holds a Ph.D. in computer engineering from the Scuola Superiore Sant'Anna in Pisa, Italy.

Dederations

To my parents, who raised and bore me,
to my friends, who cherished me,
and, above all,
to the girl I love.
—Claudio

To my wife Antonella, the love of my life.
—Silvano

Acknowledgments

We wish to express our thanks to the Nuova Systems and Cisco executive teams who made this book possible.

A particular thanks goes to the many engineers and marketing folks with whom we have collaborated in the recent years to develop the technologies described in this book.

We credit and appreciate Garth O'Mara, Carlos Pereira, and Landon Curt Noll for their extensive reviews of this book.

A special thanks goes to Luca Cafiero, the father of FCoE.

Our gratitude goes to Mario Mazzola, who has been our mentor and friend for all these years.

Contents

Case Studies 125

Bibliography 139

Preface

This book describes the work done by Nuova Systems and Cisco on the evolution of Ethernet as a Data Center Network in 2006 and 2007. The technologies described herein have been accepted by industry and, starting in 2008, made their way into both products and standards.

In particular, the FC-BB-5 standard, which defines Fibre Channel over Ethernet (FCoE), has been approved by the International Committee for Information Technology Standards (INCITS) T11 Fibre Channel committee on June 4, 2009, and was forwarded to INCITS for publication as an American National Standards Institute (ANSI) standard. This book reflects the FCoE standard.

This book describes new Data Center technologies with an educational view. The reader will find here updated material compliant with current standards and material part of proposals for future standards.

Standards are expected to evolve; therefore this book should not be used as a basis for designing standards-compliant products. Designers should refer always to the most recent standards when designing products.

This book probably contains errors. The authors would appreciate if you email any corrections to the following address:

dc_book@ip6.com

Chapter 1

I/O Consolidation

Introduction

Today Ethernet is by far the dominant interconnection network in the Data Center. Born as a shared media technology, Ethernet has evolved over the years to become a network based on point-to-point full-duplex links. In today's Data Centers, it is deployed at speeds of 100 Mbit/s and 1 Gbit/s, which are a reasonable match for the current I/O performance of PCI, based servers.

Storage traffic is a notable exception, because it is typically carried over a separate network built according to the Fibre Channel (FC) suite of standards. Most large Data Centers have an installed base of Fibre Channel. These FC networks (also called fabrics) are typically not large, and many separate fabrics are deployed for different groups of servers. Most Data Centers duplicate FC fabrics for high availability reasons.

In the High Performance Computing (HPC) sector and for applications that require cluster infrastructures, dedicated and proprietary networks like Myrinet and Quadrix have been deployed. A certain penetration has been achieved by Infiniband (IB), both in the HPC sector and, for specific applications, in the Data Center. Infiniband provides a good support for clusters requiring low latency and high throughput from user memory to user memory.

Figure 1-1 illustrates a common Data Center configuration with one Ethernet core and two independent SAN fabrics for availability reasons (labeled SAN A and SAN B).

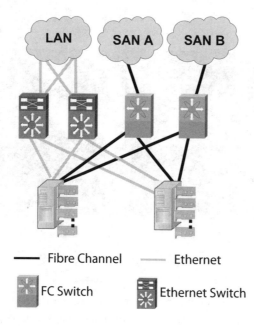

Figure 1-1   Current Data Center Architecture

What Is I/O Consolidation

I/O consolidation is the capability of a switch or a host adapter to use the same physical infra-structure to carry multiple types of traffic, each typically having peculiar characteristics and specific handling requirements.

From the network side, this equates in having to install and operate a single network instead of three (see Figure 1-2). From the hosts and storage arrays side, this equates in having to purchase fewer Converged Network Adapters (CNA) instead of Ethernet NICs, FC HBAs, and IB HCAs. This requires a lower number of PCI slots on the servers, and it is particularly beneficial in the case of Blade Servers.

The benefits for the customers are

- Great reduction, simplification, and standardization of cabling
- Absence of gateways that are always a bottleneck and a source of incompatibilities
- Less need for power and cooling
- Reduced cost

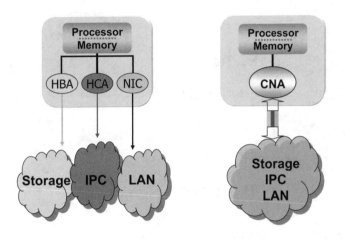

Figure 1-2   I/O Consolidation in the Network

To be viable, I/O consolidation should maintain the same management paradigm that currently applies to each traffic type.

Figure 1-3 shows an example in which 2 FC HBAs, 2 Ethernet NICs, and 2 IB HCAs are replaced by 2 CNAs.

Merging the Requirements

The biggest challenge of I/O consolidation is to satisfy the requirements of different traffic classes with a single network.

The classical LAN traffic that nowadays consists mainly of IPv4 and IPv6 traffic must run on native Ethernet [4]. Too much investment has been done in this area and too many applications assume that Ethernet is the underlying network for this to change. This traffic is characterized by a large number of flows. Typically these flows were not sensitive to latency, but this is changing rapidly, and latency now must be taken into serious consideration. Streaming Traffic is also sensitive to latency jitter.

Storage traffic must follow the Fibre Channel (FC) model. Again, large customers have massive investments in FC infrastructure and management. Storage provisioning often relies on FC services like naming, zoning, and so on. Because SCSI is extremely sensitive to packet drops, in FC losing frames is not an option. FC traffic is characterized by large frame sizes, to carry the typical 2KB SCSI payload.

Inter Processor Communication (IPC) traffic is characterized by a mix of large and small messages. It is typically latency, sensitive (especially the short messages). IPC traffic is used in

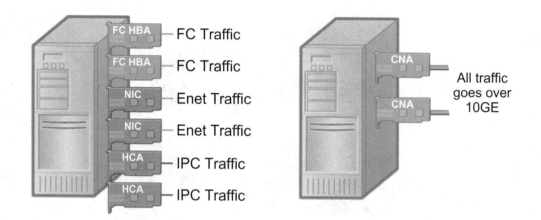

Figure 1-3   I/O Consolidation in the Servers

Clusters (i.e., interconnections of two or more computers). Examples of server clustering in the data center include

- Availability clusters (e.g., Symantec/Veritas VCS, MSCS)
- Clustered file systems
- Clustered databases (e.g., Oracle RAC)
- VMware virtual infrastructure services (e.g., VMware VMotion, VMware HA)

Clusters do not care too much about the underlying network if it is cheap, it is high bandwidth, it is low latency, and the adapters provide zero-copy mechanisms.

Why I/O Consolidation Has Not Yet Been Successful

There have been previous attempts to implement I/O consolidation. Fibre Channel itself was proposed as an I/O consolidation network, but its poor support for multicast/broadcast traffic never made it credible.

Infiniband has also attempted I/O consolidation with some success in the HPC world. It has not penetrated a larger market due to its lack of compatibility with Ethernet (again, no good multicast/broadcast support) and with FC (it uses a storage protocol that is different from FC) and to the need of gateways that are bottlenecks and incompatibility points.

iSCSI has been probably the most significant attempt at I/O consolidation. Up to now it has been limited to the low performance servers, mainly because Ethernet had a maximum speed of 1 Gbit/s. This limitation has been removed by 10 Gigabit Ethernet (10GE), but there are concerns that the TCP termination required by iSCSI is onerous at the 10Gbit/s speed. The real downside is that iSCSI is "SCSI over TCP," it is not "FC over TCP," and therefore it does not preserve the management and deployment model of FC. It still requires gateways, and it has a different naming scheme (perhaps a better one, but anyhow different), a different way of doing zoning, and so on.

Fundamental Technologies

The two technologies that will play a big role in enabling I/O consolidation are PCI-Express and 10 Gigabit Ethernet (10GE).

PCI-Express

Peripheral Component Interconnect (PCI) is an old standard to interconnect peripheral devices to computer that has been around for many years [1].

PCI-Express (PCI-E or PCIe) [2] is a computer expansion card interface format designed to replace PCI, PCI-X, and AGP. It removes one of the limitations that have plagued all these I/O consolidation attempts (i.e., the lack of I/O bandwidth in the server buses), and it is compatible with current operating systems.

PCIe uses point-to-point full duplex serial links called lanes. Each lane contains two pairs of wires: one to send and one to receive. Multiple lanes can be deployed in parallel: 1x means a single lane; 4x means 4 lanes.

In PCIe 1.1, the lanes run at 2.5 Gbps (2 Gbit/s at the datalink), and 16 lanes can be deployed in parallel. This supports speeds from 2 Gbit/s (1x) to 32 Gbit/s (16x). Due to protocol overhead 8x is required to support a 10GE interface.

PCIe 2.0 (i.e., PCIe Gen 2) doubled the bandwidth per lane from 2 Gbit/s to 4 Gbit/s and extended the maximum number of lanes to 32x. It is shipping now.

PCIe 3.0 will approximatively double the bandwidth again: "The final PCIe 3.0 specifications, including form factor specification updates, may be available by late 2009, and could be seen in products starting in 2010 and beyond." [3].

10 Gigabit Ethernet

10GE is a practical interconnection technology since 2008. The standard has reached the maturity status and cheap cabling solutions are available. Fiber continues to be used for longer distances, but copper is deployed in the Data Center for its lower cost.

Switches and CNAs have standardized their connectivity using the Small Form-factor Pluggable (SFP) transceiver. SFPs are used to interface a network device motherboard (i.e., switches, routers, or CNAs) to a fiber optic or copper cable. SFP is a popular industry format supported by several component vendors. It has expanded to become SFP+, which supports data rates up to 10 Gbit/s [9]. Applications of SFP+ include 8GFC and 10GE.

The key benefits of SFP+ are:

- A comparable panel density as SFP
- A lower module power than XENPAK, X2, and XFP
- A Nominal 1W power consumption (optional 1.5W high power module)
- Backward compatibility with SFP optical modules

The IEEE standard for twisted pair cabling (10GBASE-T) is not yet a practical interconnection technology, because it requires an enormous number of transistors, especially when the distance grows toward 100 meters (328 feet). This translates to significant power requirements and into additional delay (see Figure 1-4). Imagine trying to cool a switch linecard that has 48 10GBASE-T ports on the front-panel, each consuming 4 watts!

Technology	Cable	Distance	Power (each side)	Transceiver Latency (link)
SFP+ Cu Copper	Twinax	10m	0.1W	0.1μs
SFP+ USR ultra short reach	MM OM2 MM OM3	10m 100m	1W	0
SFP+ SR short reach	MM 62.5μm MM 50μm	82m 300m	1W	0
10GBASE-T	Cat6 Cat6a/7 Cat6a/7	55m 100m 30m	8W 8W 4W	2.5μs 2.5μs 1.5μs

Figure 1-4   Evolution of Ethernet Physical Media

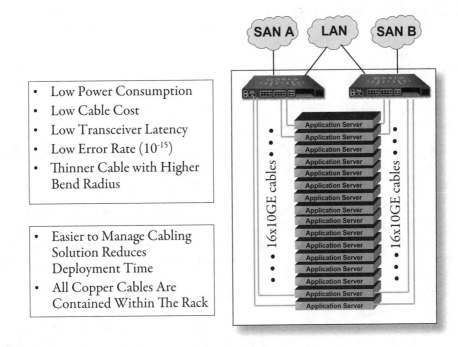

- Low Power Consumption
- Low Cable Cost
- Low Transceiver Latency
- Low Error Rate (10^{-15})
- Thinner Cable with Higher Bend Radius

- Easier to Manage Cabling Solution Reduces Deployment Time
- All Copper Cables Are Contained Within The Rack

Figure 1-5　Twinax Copper Cable

A more practical solution in the Data Center, at the rack level, is to use SFP+ with copper Twinax cable (defined in SFF-8431, see [9]). The cable is flexible, approximately 6 mm (1/4 of an inch) in diameter, and it uses the SFP+ themselves as the connectors. Cost is limited; power consumption and delay are negligible. It is limited to 10 meters (33 feet) that are sufficient to connect a few racks of servers to a common top of the rack switch.

These cables are available from Cisco, Amphenol, Molex, Panduit, and others.

Figure 1-5 illustrates the advantages of using Twinax cable inside a rack or few racks.

The cost of the transmission media is only one of the factors that need to be addressed to manufacture 10GE ports that are cost competitive. Other factors are the size of the switch buffers, and Layer 2 versus Layer 3/4 functionality.

Additional Requirements

Buffering Requirements

Buffering is a complex topic, related to propagation delays, higher level protocols, congestion control schemes, and so on. For the purpose of this discussion, it is possible to divide the networks into two classes: lossless networks and lossy networks.

This classification does not consider losses due to transmission errors that, in a controlled environment with limited distances like the Data Center, are rare in comparison to losses due to congestion.

Fibre Channel and Infiniband are examples of lossless networks (i.e., they have a link level signaling mechanism to keep track of buffer availability at the other end of the link). This mechanism allows the sender to send a frame only if a buffer is available in the receiver, and therefore the receiver never needs to drop frames. Although this seems attractive at a first glance, a word of caution is in order: Lossless networks require to be engineered in simple and limited topologies. In fact, congestion at a switch can propagate upstream throughout the network, ultimately affecting flows that are not responsible for the congestion. If circular dependencies exist, the network may experience severe deadlock and/or livelock conditions that can significantly reduce the performance of the network or destroy its functionality. These two phenomena are well known in literature and easy to reproduce in real networks. This should not discourage the potential user, since Data Center networks have simple and well-defined topologies.

Historically Ethernet has been a lossy network, since Ethernet switches do not use any mechanism to signal to the sender that they are out of buffers. A few years ago, IEEE 802.3 added a PAUSE mechanism to Ethernet. This mechanism can be used to stop the sender for a period of time, but pragmatically this feature has not been successfully deployed. Today it is common practice to drop frames when an Ethernet switch is congested. Several clever ways of dropping frames and managing queues have been proposed under the general umbrella of Active Queue Management (AQM), but they do not eliminate frame drops and require large buffers to work effectively. The most used AQM scheme is probably Random Early Detection (RED).

Avoiding frame drops is mandatory for carrying native storage traffic over Ethernet, since storage traffic does not tolerate frame drops. SCSI was designed with the assumption of running over a reliable transport in which failures are so rare that it is acceptable to recover slowly from them.

Fibre Channel is the primary protocol used to carry storage traffic, and it avoids frame drops through a link flow control mechanism based on credits called buffer-to-buffer flow control (also known as buffer-to-buffer credit or B2B credit). iSCSI is an alternative to Fibre Channel that solves the same problem by requiring TCP to recover from frame drops; however iSCSI has not been widely deployed in the Data Center.

In general, it is possible to say that lossless networks require fewer buffers in the switches than lossy networks and that these buffers may be accommodated on-chip (cheaper and faster), although large buffers require off-chip memory (expensive and slower).

Both behaviors have advantages and disadvantages. Ethernet needs to be extended to support the capability to partition the physical link into multiple logical links (by extending the IEEE 802.1Q Priority concept) and to allow lossless/lossy behavior on a per Priority basis.

Finally, it should be noted that when buffers are used they increase latency (see page 10).

Layer 2 Only

A significant part of the cost of a 10GE inter-switch port is related to functionalities above Layer 2, namely IPv4/IPv6 routing, multicast forwarding, various tunneling protocols, Multi-Protocol Label Switching (MPLS), Access Control Lists (ACLs), and deep packet inspection (Layer 4 and above). These features require external components like RAMs, CAMs, or TCAMs that significantly increase the port cost.

Virtualization, Cluster, and HPC often require extremely good Layer 2 connectivity. Virtual Machines are typically moved inside the same IP subnet (Layer 2 domain), often using a Layer 2 mechanism like gratuitous ARP. Cluster members exchange large volumes of data among themselves and often use protocols that are not IP-based for membership, ping, keep-alive, and so on.

A 10GE solution that is wire-speed, low-latency, and completely Ethernet compliant is therefore a good match for the Data Center, even if it does not scale outside the Data Center itself. Layer 2 domains of 64,000 to 256,000 members are able to satisfy the Data Center requirement for the next few years.

To support multiple independent traffic types on the same network, it is crucial to maintain the concept of Virtual LANs and to expand the concept of Priorities (see page 20).

Switch Architecture

This section deals with the historical debate of store-and-forward versus cut-through switching. Many readers may correctly complain of having heard this debate repeatedly, with some of the players switching sides over the course of the years, and they are right!

When the speed of Ethernet was low (e.g., 10 or 100 Mbit/s), this debate was easy to win for the store-and-forward camp, since the serialization delay was the dominating one. Today, with 10GE available and 40GE and 100GE in our close future, the serialization delay is low enough to justify looking at this topic again. For example, a 1-KB frame requires approximately 1 microsecond to be serialized at the speed of 10 Gbit/s.

Today many Ethernet switches are designed with a store-and-forward architecture, since this is a simpler design. Store-and-forward adds several serialization delays inside the switch and therefore the overall latency is negatively impacted [10].

Cut-through switches have a lower latency at the cost of a more complex design, required to save the intermediate store-and-forward. This is possible to achieve on fixed configuration switches like the Nexus 5000, but much more problematic on modular switches with a high port count like the Nexus 7000.

In fixed configuration switches a single speed (for example 10 Gbit/s) is used in the design of all the components, a limit to the number of ports is selected (typically less than 128), and these simplified assumptions make cut-through possible.

In modular switches, backplane switching fabrics are multiple (also to improve high availability, modularity, and serviceability) and run dedicated links toward the linecards at a speed as high as possible. Modular switches may have thousands of ports because they may have a high number of linecards and a high number of ports per linecard. The linecards are heterogeneous (1GE, 10GE, 40GE, etc.), and the speed of the front panel ports is lower than the speed of the backplane (fabric) ports. Therefore, a store and forward between the ingress linecard and the fabric and a second one between the fabric and the egress linecard are almost impossible to avoid.

Cut-through switching is not possible if there are frames already queued for a given destination and if the speed of the egress link is higher than the speed of the ingress link (data underrun). Cut-through is typically not performed for multicast/broadcast frames.

Finally, cut-through switches cannot discard corrupted frames, since when they detect that a frame is currupted, by examining the Frame Control Sequence (FCS), they have already started transmitting that frame.

Low Latency

The latency parameter that cluster users care about is the latency incurred in transferring a buffer from the user memory space of one computer to the user memory space of another computer. The main factors that contribute to the latency are

1. The time elapsed between the moment in which the application posts the data and the moment in which the first bit starts to flow on the wire. This is determined by the zero-copy mechanism and by the capability of the NIC to access the data directly in host memory, even if this is scattered in physical memory. To keep this time low most NICs today use DMA scatter/gather operations to efficiently move frames between the memory and the NIC. This in turn is influenced by the type of protocol offload used (i.e., stateless versus TOE [TCP Offload Engine]).

2. Serialization delay: This depends only on the link speed. For example, at 10 Gbit/s the serialization of one Kbyte requires 0.8 microseconds.

3. Propagation delay: This is similar in copper and fiber; it is typically 2/3 of the speed of light and can be rounded to 200 meters/microsecond one way or to 100 meters/microsecond round-trip delay. Some people prefer to express it as 5 nanoseconds/meter, and this is correct as well. In published latency data, the propagation delay is always assumed to be zero. The size of Data Center networks must be limited to a few hundreds meters to keep low this delay, otherwise it becomes dominant and low latency cannot be achieved.

4. Switch latency varies in the presence or absence of congestion. Under congestion the switch latency is mainly due to the buffering occurring inside the switch and low latency cannot be achieved. In a noncongested situation the latency depends mainly on the switch architecture, as explained on page 9.

5. Same as in point 1, but on the receiving side.

Native Support for Storage Traffic

The term native support for storage traffic indicates the capability of a network to act as a transport for the SCSI protocol. Figure 1-6 illustrates possible alternative SCSI transports.

SCSI was designed assuming the underlying physical layer was a short parallel cable, internal to the computer, and therefore extremely reliable. Based on this assumption, SCSI is not efficient in recovering from transmission errors. A frame loss may cause SCSI to time-out and recover in up to one minute.

For this reason, when the need arose to move the storage out of the servers in the storage arrays, the Fibre Channel protocol was chosen as a transport for SCSI. Fibre Channel, through its buffer-to-buffer (B2B) credit-based flow control scheme, guarantees the same frame delivery reliability of the SCSI parallel bus and therefore is a good match for SCSI.

Ethernet does not have a credit-based flow control scheme, but it does have a PAUSE mechanism. A proper implementation of the PAUSE mechanism achieves results identical to a credit-based flow control scheme, in a distance-limited environment like the Data Center.

To support I/O consolidation (i.e., to avoid interference between different classes of traffic) PAUSE needs to be extended per Priority (see page 20).

RDMA Support

Cluster applications require two message types:

■ Short synchronization messages among cluster nodes with minimum latency.

■ Large messages to transfer buffers from one node to another without CPU intervention. This is also referred to as Remote Direct Memory Access (RDMA).

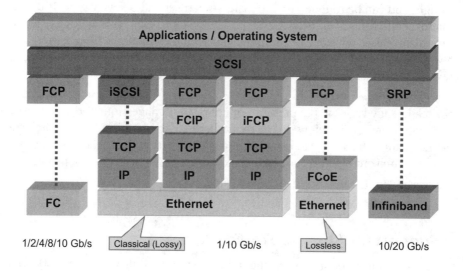

Figure 1-6 SCSI Transports

In the latter case the buffer resides in the user memory (rather than in the kernel) of a process. The buffer must be transferred to the user memory of another process. User memory is virtual memory, and it is therefore scattered in physical memory.

The RDMA operation must happen without CPU intervention, and therefore the NIC must be able to accept a command to transfer a user buffer, gather it from physical memory, implement a reliable transport protocol, and transfer it to the other NIC. The receiving NIC must verify the integrity of the data, signal the successful transfer or the presence of errors, and scatter the data in the destination host physical memory without CPU intervention.

RDMA requires in-order reliable delivery of its messages by the underlying transport.

In the IP world, there is no assumption on the reliability of the underlying network. iWARP (Internet Wide Area RDMA Protocol) is an Internet Engineering Task Force (IETF) update of the RDMA Consortium's RDMA over TCP standard. iWARP is layered above TCP, which guarantees in-order delivery. Packets dropped by the underlying network are recovered by TCP through retransmission.

Over networks with limited scope, such as Data Center networks, in-order frame delivery can be achieved without using a heavy protocol such as TCP. As an example, in-order frame delivery is successfully achieved by Fibre Channel fabrics and Ethernet networks.

As discussed in Chapter 2, Ethernet can be extended to become lossless. In Lossless Ethernet dropping happens only because of catastrophic events, like transmission errors or topology reconfigurations. The RDMA protocol may therefore be designed with the assumption that frames are normally delivered in order without any frame being lost. Protocols like LLC2, HDLC, LAPB, and so on work well if the frames are delivered in order and if the probability of frame drop is low.

Lossless Ethernet can also be integrated with a congestion control mechanism at Layer 2.

Another important requirement for RDMA is the support of standard APIs. Among the many proposed, RDS, IB verbs, SDP, and MPI seem the most interesting. RDS is used in the database community and MPI is widely adopted in the HPC market.

Open Fabrics Alliance (OFED) is currently developing a unified, open-source software stack for the major RDMA fabrics.

Chapter 2

Enabling Technologies

Introduction

Ethernet needs to be enhanced to be a viable solution for I/O consolidation. This section describes the required enhancements.

Lossless Ethernet

The term lossless Ethernet has been recently introduced to indicate an implementation of Ethernet bridges (i.e., switches) that do not lose frames under congestion.

Three questions come to mind immediately...plus one:

- Can Ethernet be lossless?
- Is a credit scheme required?
- Is lossless better?
  ...plus...
- Is anything else required?

PAUSE

Historically, there have been three possible causes of frames drop in Ethernet:

- **Frame Errors:** A frame is received with an incorrect FCS (CRC). These errors are rare and can be recovered only by a higher-level protocol. The probabilities of a frame error in Fibre Channel and in Ethernet are the same at the same speed: Fibre Channel accepts rare frame errors and so does Ethernet. This is not a factor in Data Center environments.

- **Collisions:** A frame cannot be transmitted due to multiple collisions during the transmission attempts. Collisions were possible in Ethernet with shared media. With the advent of Fast Ethernet (100 Mbit/s) IEEE 802.3 introduced full duplex links. Full duplex is the only modality supported in 10GE and it does not have collisions, since a transmission media is dedicated per each direction and it is always available.

- **Congestion in switches that causes buffers overflow:** This is avoided in Fibre Channel by using buffer-to-buffer credits (see page 17). The equivalent mechanism in Ethernet is the PAUSE mechanism defined in IEEE 802.3 – Annex 31B [4]. The PAUSE operation is used to inhibit transmission of data frames for a specified period of time when a switch queue (buffer) is full (see Figure 2-1).

Therefore, a proper implementation of the Ethernet PAUSE may transform an Ethernet network into a lossless network.

A PAUSE frame is a standard Ethernet frame, not tagged. (For example, the pausing does not apply per VLAN or per Priority, but to the whole link.) The format of a PAUSE frame is shown in Figure 2-2.

The PAUSE frame belongs to the category of MAC Control Frames that are identified by Ethertype = 0x8808. In this category the PAUSE frame is identified by the Opcode = 0x0001. The only significant field is the Pause_Time that contains the time the link needs to remain paused, expressed in Pause Quanta (512 bit times). If the link needs to remain paused for a long time, it is customary to refresh the pause by sending periodic PAUSE frames. It is also possible to send a PAUSE frame with Pause_Time = 0 to unpause the link (i.e., restart transmission, without waiting for the timer to expire).

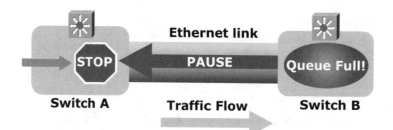

Figure 2-1   Ethernet PAUSE

PAUSE Frame

01:80:C2:00:00:01
Source Station MAC
Ethertype = 0x8808
Opcode = 0x0001
Pause_Time
Pad 42 bytes . . .
CRC

Figure 2-2   PAUSE Frame Format

Credits Versus PAUSE

Common questions are "Is PAUSE equivalent to credits?", and "Are credits better?"

Credits are used in Fibre Channel to implement lossless behavior. On each link, at link initialization, the number of buffers is pre-agreed, and each link end-point keeps an account of the free buffers. Let us consider the link in Figure 2-3. Switch A is the sender, and it can transmit a frame only if there is at least one free buffer available in switch B. In the case shown in Figure 2-3, there are not free buffers in B, because the buffer-to-buffer (B2B) count is zero, and therefore Switch A has to wait until Switch B sends a R_RDY (Receiver Ready) to switch A, indicating that a buffer has freed up. R_RDY is an ordered set. (That is, a special Fibre Channel transmission word that is transmitted between frames and that indicates the availability of a new buffer.)

With PAUSE (see Figure 2-1) Switch A does not keep track of the buffers available in Switch B, and it assumes by default that buffers are available, unless told the contrary by switch B with a PAUSE frame. PAUSE is a regular Ethernet frame and therefore it uses slightly more bandwidth than the credit mechanism, negligible in comparison to the data transferred.

Although the technicalities of buffer-to-buffer credits are different from PAUSE, the observable behavior is the same, especially in Data Center environments where the propagation delays are limited.

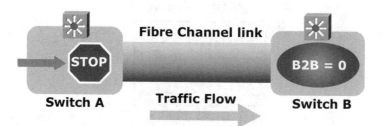

Figure 2-3   Buffer-to-Buffer Credits

It should be noticed that for I/O consolidation PFC (see page 20) is superior to the basic FC credits mechanism, since FC credits apply to the whole link and not per Priority.

FC credits have been extended with a new ordered set called VC_RDY (Virtual Circuit Ready) to provide a similar functionality.

PAUSE Propagation

Another question that is often asked is: "How does PAUSE propagate in the network?"

PAUSE, PFC, and Credits are all hop-by-hop mechanisms. (That is, they apply to a specific link.) They do not automatically propagate to other links in the network.

The goal of these three mechanisms is to suspend the transmission of frames so that the receiver is not forced to drop frames if it cannot forward them due to congestion.

Let us consider the diagram in Figure 2-4. Let us assume that switch S3 becomes congested and it issues a PAUSE toward switch S2. S2 suspends transmission and starts to build a queue. When the queue exceeds a given threshold, S2 is forced to send a PAUSE to S1 to avoid dropping frames.

Therefore there is not a direct propagation of the PAUSE mechanism in the network, but there may be an indirect propagation: PAUSE is generated–queue gets full–PAUSE is generated–queue gets full–and so on.

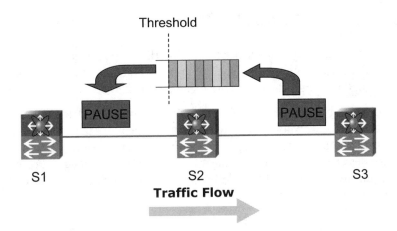

Threshold

PAUSE   PAUSE

S1   S2   S3

Traffic Flow

Figure 2-4   PAUSE Propagation

Is Lossless Better?

This is a complex topic, partially discussed in page 8. Lossless has advantages and disadvantages.

On the plus side, frames are never dropped, and therefore higher-level protocols have a reduced amount of work to do. This is particularly important for protocols like SCSI that are not good at error recovery. Lossless is therefore important for transporting FC over Ethernet. Other application level protocols may take advantage of a lossless behavior, for example Network File System (NFS).

In the case of TCP the fast retransmission takes care of most of the frame losses, but the initial and final frames of the flow are not protected, and also the intermediate one may suffer in the presence of severe congestion. Therefore, very short TCP flows have been shown to work better on lossless Ethernet.

On the neutral side, TCP relies on losses to adjust its windows, and therefore dropping frames is a commonly used technique by Active Queue Management (AQM) systems like Random Early Detection (RED) to signal congestion to TCP.

On the minus side, lossless can cause congestion spreading and head of line (HOL) blocking and, if circular dependencies exist among buffers, livelock and deadlock. This can be alleviated with techniques like BCN/QCN (see page 25). In addition, care must be taken in configuring the links consistently. A protocol such as DCBX (see page 22) solves this issue.

Why PAUSE Is Not Widely Deployed

The main reason is inconsistent implementations. The IEEE 802.3 standard defined the basic mechanism but left the door open to incomplete implementations. However, this is easy to fix and is being fixed in the new products that are reaching the market.

It is important to remember that I/O consolidation requires a single link to carry multiple traffic classes. PAUSE applies to the whole link. (That is, it is a single mechanism for all traffic classes.) Often different traffic classes have incompatible requirements (e.g., some need a lossy behavior, others need a lossless behavior), and this may cause "traffic interference." For example, with the PAUSE mechanism, storage traffic could be paused due to congestion on IP traffic. This is clearly undesirable and needs to be fixed.

Priority-based Flow Control (PFC)

Priority-based Flow Control (PFC, also known as Per Priority Pause or PPP) [6], is a finer grain flow control mechanism. IEEE 802.1Q defines a tag (shown in Figure 2-5), which contains a 3-bit Priority field. (That is, it can encode eight priorities.) PFC enables PAUSE functionality on a per-Priority basis.

If separate traffic classes are mapped to different priorities, there is no traffic interference. For example, in Figure 2-6, storage traffic is mapped to Priority three and it is paused, while IPC traffic is mapped to Priority six and it is being forwarded and so is IP traffic, that is mapped to Priority one.

PFC requires a more complex organization in the data plane with dedicated resources (e.g., buffers, queues) per Priority.

PFC is based on a public proposal by Cisco that has a high level of industry support and that became the basis for the 802.1Qbb project [6] in the IEEE 802.1 Data Center Bridging task group (see [5]).

The PFC Frame format is shown in Figure 2-7 and it is similar to the PAUSE frame.

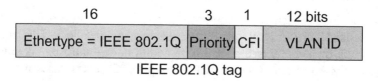

Figure 2-5   IEEE 802.1Q Tag with the Priority Field

Transmit Queues
Ethernet Link
Receive Queues
One
Two
Three
STOP
PAUSE
Four
Five
Six
Seven
Eight
One
Two
Three
Four
Five
Six
Seven
Eight
Switch A
Switch B
Eight Priorities

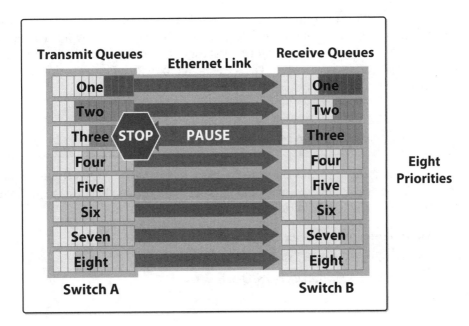

Figure 2-6 PFC (Priority-based Flow Control)

Priority-based Flow Control
01:80:C2:00:00:01
Source Station MAC
Ethertype = 0x8808
Opcode = 0x0101
Class enable vector
Time (class 0)
Time (class 1)
Time (class 2)
Time (class 3)
Time (class 4)
Time (class 5)
Time (class 6)
Time (class 7)
Pad
28 bytes
...
CRC

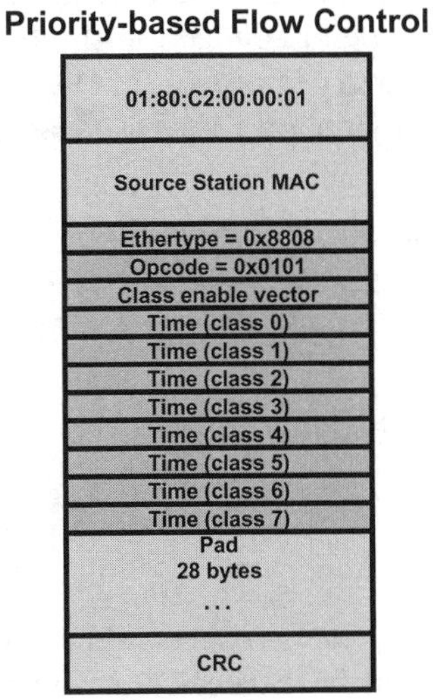

Figure 2-7 PFC Frame Format

The Ethertype = 0x8808 is the same as for PAUSE (MAC Control Frame), but the Opcode = 0x0101 is different. There are eight Time fields, one per Priority. To allow for flexible implementation, PFC frames may carry time information for one Priority, for a few Priorities, or for all Priorities. This is achieved by having a Class enable vector with a bit per each Priority. For a given Priority, the bit indicates if the Time field is valid.

Additional Components

What we have discussed up to this point is the basic techniques required to implement I/O consolidation. Additional techniques make I/O consolidation deployable on a larger scale. The next sections describe the following additional components:

- Discovery Protocol (i.e., DCBX)
- Bandwidth Manager (i.e., ETS)
- Congestion Management (i.e., BCN/QCN)

DCBX: Data Center Bridging eXchange

DCBX derives its name from the IEEE 802.1 Data Center Bridging task group (see [5]), which deals with most of the Ethernet extensions described in this document. DCBX is the management protocol of Data Center Bridging, defined in the IEEE 802.1Qaz project [7]. DCBX is an extension of Link Layer Discovery Protocol (LLDP, see IEEE 802.1AB-2005). LLDP is a vendor-neutral Layer 2 protocol that allows a network device to advertise its identity and its capabilities on the local network.

DCBX provides hop-by-hop support for

- Priority-based Flow Control (PFC)
- Bandwidth Management (ETS)
- Congestion Management (BCN/QCN)
- Applications (e.g., FCoE)
- Logical Link Down

DCBX discovers the capabilities of the two peers at the two ends of a link and can check that they are consistent. DCBX can notify the device manager in the case of configuration mismatches and can provide basic configuration if one of the two peers is not configured.

Figure 2-8 shows a deployment scenario for a network that is using DCBX. DCBX-capable links exchange DCB capabilities, and conflict alarms are sent to the appropriate management stations. As an example, a boundary is shown indicating which devices support Congestion Management and which ones do not.

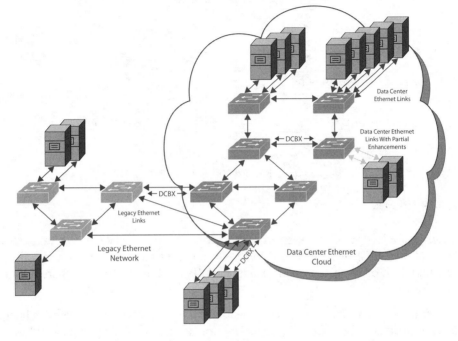

Figure 2-8   DCBX Deployment

Bandwidth Management

IEEE 802.1Q-2005 defines eight Priorities but not a simple, effective, and consistent scheduling mechanism to process them. The scheduling goals are typically bandwidth, latency, and jitter control.

Products typically implement some form of Deficit Weighted Round Robin (DWRR), but there is no consistency across implementations, and therefore configuration and interworking is problematic.

IEEE 802.1 DCB [5] is defining, in the 802.1Qaz project [7], a mechanism for a hardware efficient two-level DWRR mechanism with strict Priority support, called Enhanced Transmission Selection (ETS).

Figure 2-9 shows how, with ETS, Priorities are grouped in Priority Groups with a first level of scheduling and then the Priority Groups are scheduled by a second level scheduler.

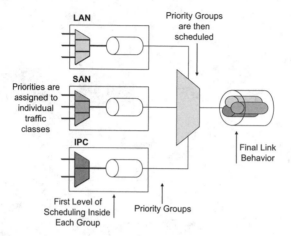

Figure 2-9   Priority Groups

With this structure it is possible to assign bandwidth to each Priority Group (e.g., 40% LAN, 40% SAN, and 20% IPC). Within each Priority Group, multiple traffic classes are allowed to share the bandwidth of the group. (For example, VoIP and bulk traffic can share 40% of the LAN bandwidth.)

This architecture allows to control not only bandwidth but also latency. Latency is becoming increasingly important in Data Centers, especially for IPC applications (see page 10).

An example of link bandwidth allocation is shown in Figure 2-10.

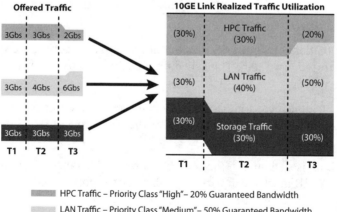

Figure 2-10   Example of Bandwidth Management

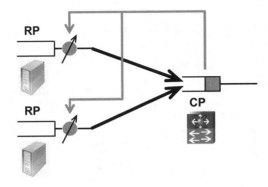

Figure 2-11   Congestion Point and Reaction Points

Congestion Management

One of the downsides of lossless Ethernet discussed in page 19 is that, in presence of congestion, it tends to create undesirable Head Of Line (HOL) blocking. This is because it spreads the congestion across the network.

IEEE 802.1 DCB [5] is defining, in the 802.1Qau project [8], a Layer 2 end-to-end congestion notification protocol. The idea behind this effort is to move the congestion from the core to the edges of the network to avoid congestion spreading. At the edge of the network, congestion is easier to deal with, since the number of flows is much lower than in the core, and therefore the flows that cause congestion can be easily isolated and rate limited.

The algorithms that have been considered are Backward Congestion Notification (BCN) and Quantized Congestion Notification (QCN), with QCN being standardized. They are similar, and they act as shown in Figure 2-11.

When congestion notification is used, a congested switch (i.e., the Congestion Point or CP) sends messages toward the source of the congestion (i.e., the Reaction Points or RP) to signal its congested state and that a rate reduction through shaping the traffic entering the network is needed.

On receiving congestion notification messages, a rate limiter is installed as close as possible to the source of the congestion, possibly in the host generating the flow. This alleviates the congestion in the core without causing congestion spreading.

The main difference between this kind of signaling and PAUSE is that PAUSE is hop-by-hop (see page 18), while these congestion notification messages propagate all the way toward the source of the congestion (see Figure 2-12).

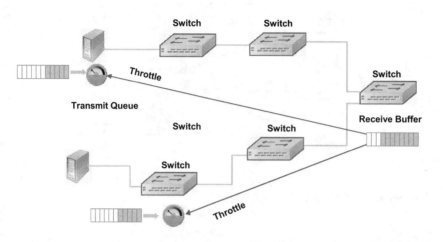

Figure 2-12 Backward Signaling

The rate limiter parameters are dynamically adjusted based on feedback coming from congestion points. This is similar to what TCP does at the transport layer (Layer 4 of the ISO OSI model), but it is implemented at Layer 2 and therefore it applies to all traffic types, not just TCP. The algorithm used is an Additive Increase, Multiplicative Decrease (AIMD) rate control. In absence of congestion it increases the bandwidth linearly, but in presence of congestion it decreases it exponentially. (For example, the bandwidth is halved.) A similar scheme is implemented for Fibre Channel in the MDS switches and it is called Fibre Channel Congestion Control (FCC).

Delayed Drop

Delayed Drop is a means of using PFC or PAUSE to mitigate the effects of short-term traffic bursts while maintaining frame drops for long-term congestion.

Delayed Drop allows a buffer of a switch to virtually extend to the previous hop. With PFC this is enabled per Priority, and it is particularly useful on the lossy Priorities to reduce frames drop for transient congestions. It is implemented by asserting PFC on the Priority for a limited period.

One of the motivations behind Delayed Drop is the limited amount of buffer available in the switches (see page 8). Being capable of borrowing buffer space from the previous switch may allow absorbing a transient congestion (e.g., an isolated burst) without dropping frames on a lossy priority.

When the limited period expires, either the burst has been absorbed, and the traffic flows normally again, or frames are dropped as in regular Ethernet.

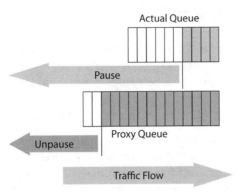

Figure 2-13   Delayed Drop and Proxy Queue

Figure 2-13 shows a possible implementation of Delayed Drop using a proxy queue to measure the duration of traffic bursts. During normal operation, when frames are added or drained, the proxy queue (that does not really exist, it is just a set of counters) mimics the actual queue. When a burst of traffic is received, the actual queue fills to its high-water mark and issues a PAUSE or PFC to stop incoming frames. The proxy queue, that is significantly larger than the actual queue, simulates the continued receipt of frames. When the proxy queue is filled, the PAUSE or PFC is released (i.e., a PAUSE or PFC frame with a zero Time is generated), and this, in turn, causes frames drop, because the transmitter is now allowed to transmit while the actual queue is full. This behavior is summarized in Table 2-1.

In other words, during short-term congestion both queues drain fast enough that the actual queue releases the PAUSE on its own. During long-term congestion, the proxy queue fills to its high-water mark, and it releases the PAUSE. The actual queue begins to drop packets, and the congestion is managed through higher-level protocols.

Table 2-1   Delayed Drop Actions

Actual Queue	Proxy Queue
Adds a frame	Adds a frame
Issues a PAUSE or PFC	Adds frames at line rate
Drains a frame	Drains a frame
Is empty	Drains frames at line rate, until empty

Going Beyond Spanning Tree

Layer 2 networks forward frames along spanning trees built by the Spanning Tree Protocol (STP). The STP takes a meshed network and reduces it to a tree by pruning some links. This technique has been used for as long as Ethernet has existed and IEEE 802.1 has improved it over the years in different ways, for example supporting multiple, independent trees, as in the case of per VLAN Spanning Tree (PVST), and reducing the STP convergence time.

One of the primary design goals of the STP is to eliminate all loops from the network topology. This is because Ethernet frames do not contain any "time to live" data in the frame header, making it theoretically possible for frames to circulate forever in the case of topologies with loops or multiple links between devices. Moreover, it is best practice to design Layer 2 networks with looped topologies, as multiple redundant physical links are deployed between access/distribution and distribution/core layers to protect against the failure in any one physical path. This issue is further compounded by the mechanism used by Ethernet bridges/switches to determine forwarding paths for frames.

Ethernet bridges/switches learn the location of destination MAC addresses by monitoring the source MAC addresses contained in the frame header (a mechanism called backward learning). When a source MAC address is seen, the location of that device is learned, and frames can be forwarded directly toward that device via the appropriate spanning tree. However, in the case of destination addresses that have not yet been learned, frames are flooded on all ports (except the receiving port). In absence of the STP, this flooding process can create data storms in looped network environments, as frames are replicated and flooded by each bridge or switch in the network. The same applies for Multicast/Broadcast traffic.

Alternative models have been proposed at Layer 2 but, up to now, they have not been successful. Nonetheless, many customers continue to ask for alternative solutions that are scalable and reliable.

The limitation of the STP can be understood by looking at the anatomy of a tree; see Figure 2-14.

The branches are smaller toward the leaves and bigger toward the roots. The trunk needs to be the biggest since it needs to carry the sap up to all the leaves.

The same concept can be explained more formally by looking at the topology of Figure 2-15 that illustrates a meshed network that has been reduced to a tree by the STP. At each level the network has 16 x 10GE links for a total of 160 Gbps of aggregated bandwidth. However. most links are blocked by the STP protocol and the usable bandwidth is reduced from 160 Gbps to 40 Gbps, when going from the access to the distribution layer, and from 40 Gbps to 20 Gbps, when going from the distribution layer to the core.

Today, in the Data Center, the "Ethernet branches" have all the same size as the trunk (i.e., 10 Gbps). Servers connect to the tree with 10GE ports and the backbone links are also 10GE.

California Black Oak Tree
Silvano Gai
June 2009

Figure 2-14 Anatomy of a Tree

This is clearly undesirable, since it creates congestion near the root and it limits the "bisectional bandwidth" of the network.

Bisectional bandwidth is the most common measure of aggregate bandwidth and is loosely defined as follows: "If you divide the hosts of a network in two groups of equal size, the two groups will be interconnected by some network links. The bisectional bandwidth is the total possible bandwidth crossing these links."

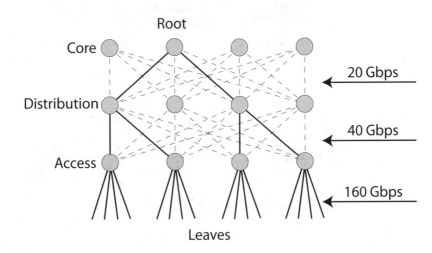

Figure 2-15 Meshed Network Reduced to a Tree

For example, in Figure 2-15, let us define the two sets as the eight left-most leaves and the eight right-most leaves. The bisectional bandwidth is then 10 Gbps (the links incoming and outgoing from the root).

This is because the switching capacity greatly exceeds the transmission capacity. We are capable of building single chip Terabit switches, but we are not capable of transmitting faster than 10 Gbps. Even with the advent of 40GE (late 2010) and 100GE (late 2011), the situation will not change much.

Another reason why customers do not like Spanning Tree is that all the links connected to blocked ports sit unused in standby mode. Instead Layer 2 multipath avoids having unused links (all the links forward), and it also allows for more direct paths between servers, when needed.

Figure 2-16 shows a classical network topology in which half the ports that connect the access switches to the distribution switches are blocked by Spanning Tree and they are available only as standby ports. To circumvent this issue, PVST has been deployed often in the past, blocking different ports for different VLANs.

The only way to avoid ports being blocked and therefore get to an active/standby topology is to abandon the tree model and adopt an approach in which all ports are active and multiple paths between two points can be used.

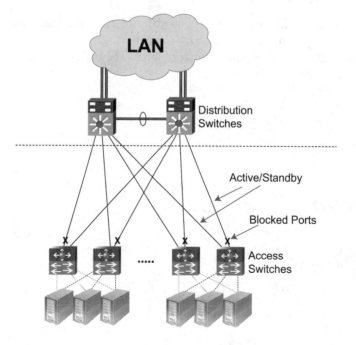

Figure 2-16   Spanning Tree Configuration with Blocked Ports

Alternative models have been proposed in products and standards to provide active-active topologies, and some are already deployed. We will discuss six of them in this section.

Four alternative models solve the important subproblem of how to provide active-active connectivity from an access switch to two core switches. They are:

- Etherchannel, see page 32
- VSS (Virtual Switching System), see page 32
- vPC (virtual Port Channel), see page 34
- Ethernet Host Virtualizer, see page 36

Two other alternative models solve the more general problem of forwarding frames in a Layer 2 meshed topology without blocking any port. They are:

- L2MP/MIM (Layer 2 Multi-Path/Mac-in-Mac), see page 47
- L2MP/TRILL (Layer 2 Multi-Path/Transparent Interconnection of Lots of Links), see page 51

Figure 2-17 contains an example of a three-tier datacenter topology in which all the links forward traffic.

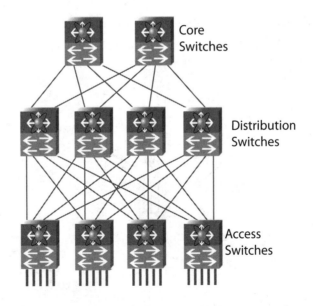

Figure 2-17   L2MP Network (L2MP/MIM or L2MP/TRILL)

Active-Active Connectivity

Etherchannel

Etherchannel is a port aggregation technology primarily introduced by Cisco in 1994 and standardized by IEEE 802 in 2000 in the project IEEE 802.3ad. It is widely implemented on Cisco and non-Cisco switches.

Etherchannel allows aggregating several physical Ethernet links to create one logical Ethernet link with a bandwidth equal to the sum of the bandwidths of the links being aggregated. Etherchannel can aggregate from two to eight links and all higher-level protocols see these multiple links as a single connection (see Figure 2-18).

This is beneficial for providing fault-tolerance and high-speed links between switches, routers, and servers, without blocking any port and therefore using all the links.

A limitation of Etherchannel is that all the physical ports in the aggregation group must reside on the same switch. For this reason the next three solutions (VSS, vPC, and Ethernet Host Virtualizer) were developed, and they are collectively illustrated in Figure 2-19.

In Figure 2-19 four access switches connect to two distribution switches and their uplinks remain active-active. (For example, the STP does not prune any link.)

Virtual Switching System (VSS)

VSS is the first of two Cisco technologies that allow using Etherchannel from an access switch to two distribution switches, as shown in Figure 2-20.

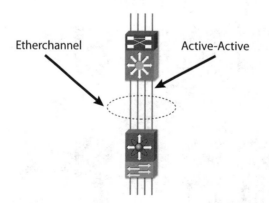

Figure 2-18   Etherchannel Between Two Switches

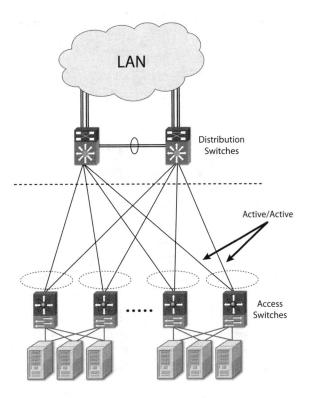

Figure 2-19 VSS, vPC, or Ethernet Host Virtualizer

VSS accomplishes this by clustering two physical chassis together into a single, logical entity. The individual chassis become indistinguishable, and therefore the access switch believes the upstream switches to be a single distribution switch, as in the case of Figure 2-18.

VSS has also many other advantages, since it improves high availability, scalability, management, and maintenance.

The key enabler of the Cisco VSS technology is a special link called Virtual Switch Link (VSL), which binds the two chassis together and passes special control information.

A VSL link is a connection between the two internal fabrics of the two switches to combine them into a single logical network entity and make them indistinguishable from an external observer. Therefore, access switches may use multiple uplinks toward the two switches and configure them as regular Etherchannel, since the VSS appears as a single, logical switch or router.

Within the Cisco VSS, both switches are active from a data plane perspective, but from the control and management plane perspective, only one switch is designated as active; the other is designated as hot-standby, much as in the case of a dual supervisor switch (e.g., the Catalyst 6500).

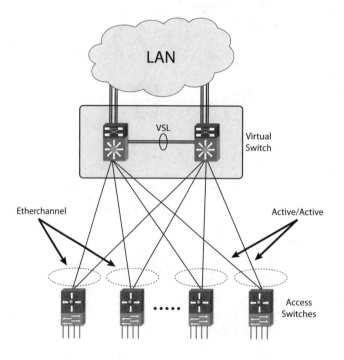

Figure 2-20   VSS

All control-plane functions, including management (SNMP, Telnet, SSH), Layer 2 protocols (STP, LACP, and so on), and Layer 3 routing protocols are centrally managed by the active switch that is also responsible for programming the hardware forwarding information of both switches.

VSS requires a tight alignment and integration of the two switches that are the members of the cluster.

virtual Port Channel (vPC)

vPC (also known as Multi-Chassis Etherchannel/virtual Port Channel, MCEC/vPC) achieves a result similar to VSS without requiring the same level of tight integration between the vPC switches (see Figure 2-21). In particular, there is not the concept of a VSL with a proprietary protocol, and the level of alignment between vPC switches is not so high as in the case of VSS.

From the access switch perspective, nothing changes: vPC continues to use an unmodified Etherchannel and sees the vPC switches as a single STP logical bridge.

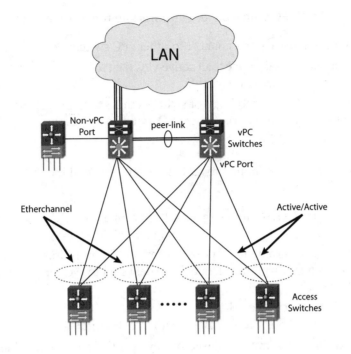

Figure 2-21   MCEC/vPC

Each vPC switch maintains its identity and its management and control planes, but it cooperates with the other vPC switch to provide active-active virtual Port Channel. It is not a goal of vPC to present the two vPC switches as a single one, as in the case of VSS.

The link between the vPC switches is called peer-link. This is a regular data link as far as control plane and data plane forwarding is concerned. In addition, this link plays an important role for

- vPC-related control plane exchanges between vPC switches
- Heartbeat mechanism between vPC switches
- Data traffic during failure scenarios
- Data traffic for asymmetrically connected hosts/switches
- Broadcast/multicast/flooded frames

The key challenge in vPC, present also in VSS, is to deliver each frame exactly once, avoiding frame duplication and loops. This must happen with some access switches that are connected to both distribution switches and some that are connected to only one (because, for example, one uplink has failed), without using Spanning Tree.

To achieve this goal each vPC switch divides its ports into three groups (see Figure 2-21):

- **Peer-link ports:** These ports connect to other vPC switches.
- **vPC ports:** These ports connect an active vPC (i.e., to hosts or switches that are connected also to the other vPC switch).
- **Non-vPC ports:** Connect to hosts or switches that are "orphan." (For example, they do not have connectivity to the other vPC switch, either as the result of configuration or as the result of a failure.)

A complete discussion of how frame forwarding works is beyond the scope of this book, but in general

- A unicast frame received from either a vPC port or a non-vPC port is forwarded as usual.
- A unicast frame received on the peer-link for a vPC port is dropped, since the receiving switch assumes that it has already been delivered to the correct destination by the other vPC switch.
- A unicast frame received on the peer-link for a non-vPC port is forwarded, since the other vPC switch did not have a direct path to deliver it.
- A multicast/broadcast frame received on any port that is not a peer-link is delivered to all the other ports.
- A multicast/broadcast frame received on a peer-link is delivered to all the non-vPC ports, since the receiving switch assumes that it has already been delivered to the vPC ports by the other vPC switch.

Ethernet Host Virtualizer

VSS and vPC are techniques implemented on the distribution switches to allow the access switches to keep using Etherchannel in a traditional manner.

The same problem can be solved on the access switches by a technique called Ethernet Host Virtualizer.

With reference to Figure 2-22, the access switches implement Ethernet Host Virtualizer while the distribution switches continue to run the classical STP.

A switch running Ethernet Host Virtualizer divides its ports into two groups: host ports and network ports. Both types of ports can be a single interface or an Etherchannel. The switch then associates each host port with a network port. This process is called pinning.

The same host port always uses the same network port, unless it fails. In this case, the access switch moves the pinning to another network port.

In the example of Figure 2-22, MAC-A is always presented on the left network port, and MAC-B is always presented on the right network port.

The decision of which network port to use for a given host port may be based on manual configuration or decided by the switch according to the load. The relationship remains intact until the host port or the network port loses connectivity.

When this happens, the associated host ports are redistributed to the remaining set of active network ports.

Particular attention must be paid to multicast and broadcast frames to avoid loops and frame duplications. Typically, access switches that implement this feature act as follows:

- They never retransmit a frame received from a network port to another network port.
- They divide the multicast/broadcast traffic according to multicast groups, and they assign each multicast group to a single network port. Only one network port may transmit and receive a multicast group.

The Ethernet Host Virtualizer is less general than the Layer 2 multipath discussed in the next section and only works for access switches that interconnect hosts or storage arrays, not for distribution or core switches. It has the big advantage of being simple to deploy and to plug into an existing core-distribution network without requiring any changes.

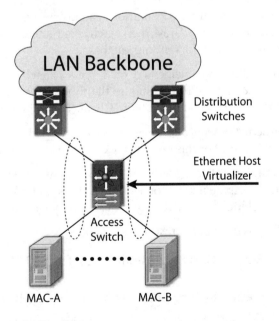

Figure 2-22   Ethernet Host Virtualizer

Layer 2 Multipath (L2MP)

L2 Multipath increases the bandwidth of L2 networks by replacing the STP with a different protocol in all the participating switches. The bisectional bandwidth increases for two reasons:

- There are no longer blocked ports and all the links are in forwarding state.
- The traffic between two points in the network can be spread among multiple paths.

Multipath is common in IP networks and is particularly important when there is limited or no differentiation in speed between access links and backbone links. As explained in Chapter 1, this is the case for Data Center networks, where initially all links are 10GE.

An additional advantage of multipath is reduced latency, since the shortest path is always used in forwarding frames, and a lower number of hops normally equates to reduced latency. In addition, a less loaded path can be used to forward delay-sensitive frames.

Multipath solutions need to provide seamless interoperability with existing protocols, in particular with the STP.

Briefly, all the Layer 2 multipath solutions require that participating switches in the network become addressable entities. This is not true in classical Ethernet switches, since the switches are transparent and never explicitly addressed (if not for management purpose). By making all the switches addressable devices, all L2MP solutions can utilize a link state protocol to compute the topology of the network (i.e., how the switches are interconnected), and from that topology they can compute a switch forwarding database.

This is similar to what is already implemented on Fibre Channel networks, where the FC switches are addressable and run FSPF to compute the topology of the network. In FC, the switch address is embedded in the FC_ID, the Fibre Channel address.

This is not the case in Ethernet. Switch addresses need to be carried in the Ethernet frames but so do the end stations addresses. For this reason an extra header is added in the L2MP cloud.

Cisco has and L2MP solution called L2MP/MIM (L2MP/MAC-In-MAC) and the IETF has a project named TRILL (Transparent Interconnection of Lots of Links [18]) defining another L2MP solution. The two solutions are extremely similar and they are explained together.

The following terminology is used in the rest of this chapter:

- With the term "DBridge" (Data Center Bridge) we refer to a L2MP/MIM-capable bridge.
- With the term "RBridge" (Routing Bridge) we refer to an L2MP/TRILL-capable bridge.
- With the term "D/RBridge" we refer to either a DBridge or an RBridge.

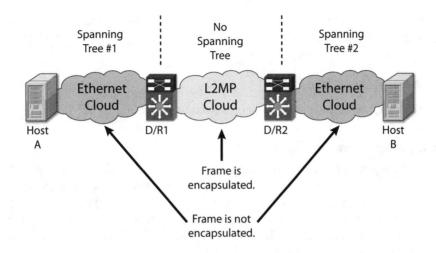

Figure 2-23 D/RBridge Forwarding in a Nutshell

To better understand how this works, let's consider the example of Figure 2-23, where Host A intends to send a frame to Host B.

The switches that sit at the edges of the L2MP cloud are called ingress/egress switches. The ingress switch (D/R1)

■ Receives the frame from the source Ethernet station (Host A)

■ Maintains a MAC table (properly a filtering database) with the addresses of the end stations learned through either backward learning or IS-IS advertisements

■ Looks up the MAC table to determine the egress switch (D/R2)

■ Adds the extra header with the address of the egress switch (Source address = D/R1, Destination Address = D/R2)

The encapsulated frame is forwarded in the core of the L2MP cloud to the egress switch looking at the egress switch address only, using the shortest path. In the L2MP cloud the addresses of the source Ethernet station (Host A) and destination Ethernet station (Host B) are ignored, since they are in the original frame that is encapsulated.

The egress switch (D/R2)

■ Removes the additional header

■ Looks up the destination Ethernet MAC (Host B) in the MAC table to determine on which port to send the frame

■ Forwards the frame to the destination Ethernet station (Host B)

On the right Ethernet cloud, one or more instances of Spanning Tree are terminated on D/R2 and not propagated by the L2MP cloud. The same is true for the left Ethernet cloud.

Basic Mechanisms in L2MP

In this section we examine the basic mechanisms required to build an L2MP solution.

Computing Routes Versus Backward Learning

Classical IEEE bridges do not explicitly compute routes to decide where to forward a frame. By default, they forward everywhere, but through a process called backward learning they build a filtering database by observing the source MAC addresses of the data frames. The filtering database is used to limit the propagation of unicast frames to a single destination. D/RBridges are designed to operate more like routers: They explicitly run a protocol to compute the forwarding paths, and they build a forwarding database among them.

Optimal Path Computation

The first issue to solve is the selection of the protocol to compute the routes (i.e., a protocol capable of identifying optimal forwarding paths for unicast and multicast) and, if they exist, equal cost multipaths (ECMP). All the modern link state protocols like OSPF, FSPF, IS-IS solve these problems by modeling the network as a graph and by applying the Dijkstra algorithm to identify the shortest paths. The solution adopted by D/RBridges is based on a Layer 2 extension of the IS-IS protocol.

Intermediate Systems to Intermediate Systems (IS-IS)

IS-IS has been chosen since it is already widely deployed on IP networks and it runs directly over Ethernet (i.e., there is no requirement to run IP), which is a desirable trait for an L2 network. The protocol was defined by the International Organization for Standardization (ISO) in the Open Systems Interconnection (OSI) protocol suite and it has been adopted by IETF with RFC 1142. IS-IS is easy to extend by defining new Type-Length-Value (TLV) attributes. Both DBridges and RBridges extend IS-IS by defining equivalent TLVs. D/RBridges use an instance of IS-IS separate from the one used by the IP protocol (L3 IS-IS). This provides better control plane separation. In fact, L3 IS-IS computes routes based on system IDs associated with L3 entities (i.e., IP routers), while L2 IS-IS does this for L2 entities (i.e., D/RBridges).

Equal Cost Multipath (ECMP)

D/RBridges are capable of load balancing traffic only over paths of equal cost (where "cost" is the metric used by IS-IS). Even if it is theoretically possible to load balance traffic over paths of nonequal cost, in both solutions this case was not considered, since it provides marginal advantages in the topologies typically used in Data Centers and it increases complexity.

Avoiding Loops (TTL)

One of the strengths of the STP is its capability to avoid loops during network reconfigurations. This is particularly critical in Layer 2 networks since there is no Time To Live (TTL) in the frame. The IS-IS protocol does not have the same goal, since IP frames (both IPv4 and IPv6) have a TTL in the IP header. The solution adopted by D/RBridges is to add a TTL in the Layer 2 header and decrement it before forwarding the frame. In DBridges this field is called TTL; in RBridges it is called Hop Count.

The TTL may also be used in a wider manner to protect against the infinite recirculation of frames. For example, a (rogue) D/RBridge erroneously or maliciously configured can create this case. In all these situations the TTL helps alleviating the issue.

In addition, an ingress check to verify which D/RBridge sourced the frame is also an important component for avoiding loops.

Hierarchical Forwarding

D/RBridges compute the shortest path and ECMPs between D/RBridges, not between end stations. Ethernet frames enter the L2MP cloud through an ingress D/RBridge and are sent to an egress D/RBridge. The D/RBridges need to know the optimal path only to other D/RBridges, not to end stations. Classical Ethernet learning is enabled only at the edge (ingress and egress) and associates the MAC addresses of end stations with the addresses of the D/RBridge where the end stations are connected. This association allows hierarchical forwarding (i.e., forwarding frames in the L2MP domain using only the D/RBridge addresses and not the end station MAC addresses). Hierarchical forwarding allows D/RBridges that are in the core and do not connect to any end stations to maintain smaller MAC forwarding tables, and therefore it is a more scalable solution.

Encapsulation

All the Layer 2 multipath solutions use some form of encapsulation. Depending on the solution, one or two additional headers are added to the basic Ethernet frame. Encapsulation has several benefits:

- It provides space for storing additional information (e.g., the TTL).

- It hides the MAC addresses in the encapsulated Ethernet frames, allowing D/RBridges to use smaller MAC address forwarding tables, since they do not need to learn all the MAC addresses of end stations.

- It may provide a separate VLAN tag for forwarding traffic between RBridges, independently from the original VLAN of the frame.

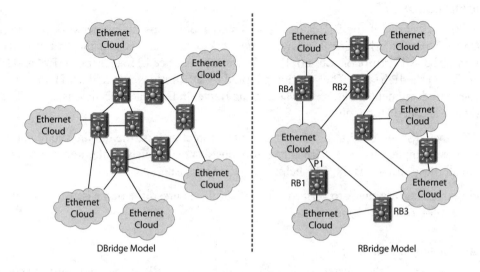

Figure 2-24   DBridge and RBridge Network Models

Connection Types

Both DBridges and RBridges can connect to legacy Ethernet switches, but while RBridges may establish an adjacency (i.e., exchange TRILL encapsulated traffic) through legacy Ethernet switches, DBridges require direct point-to-point connections. Figure 2-24 illustrates the two different models.

In the Data Center, the difference between the two models is pragmatically irrelevant, since L2MP is required in the backbone to relieve the bandwidth bottleneck. In the backbone all D/RBridges are connected by point-to-point links, and in the periphery both models support legacy Ethernet switches.

Additional Headers

The previous model difference has an impact on the number of additional headers (see Figure 2-25).

DBridges use only one additional ingress/egress header that contains the addresses of the ingress and egress DBridge, the TTL, and few other fields.

RBridges have a similar Ingress/Egress header plus a Next Hop Header used to cross the legacy Ethernet cloud that can be present between two RBridges. For example, in Figure 2-24, the RBridge RB1 can reach through P1 RBridges RB2, RB3, and RB4. RB1 selects which RBridge to send the frame by writing the appropriate MAC address in the Next Hop Header Destination

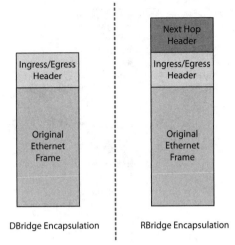

Figure 2-25 Additional Headers

MAC Address. DBridges do not have this issue, since each L2MP port is directly connected only to another DBridge.

Addressing

DBridges write in the ingress/egress header the addresses of the ingress and egress DBridges and they do not need a next hop address, since the next DBridge is always directly connected. RBridges do the same plus they write the address of the next hop RBridge in the Next Hop Header. This is necessary to avoid frames duplication when the next hop RBridge is not directly connected to the current RBridge or shared connections are used.

Frame Types

D/RBridges deal with two frame types: known unicast frames and multidestination frames. Known unicast frames are unicast frames that are destined to an Ethernet station whose location is known and therefore need to be delivered only to a specific egress D/RBridge. This includes the bulk of unicast traffic. Multidestination frames are either unknown unicast frames (i.e., unicast frames for an Ethernet station whose location is unknown) or multicast/broadcast frames. They are called multidestination, since they need to be delivered to more than one egress D/RBridge and potentially to all of them.

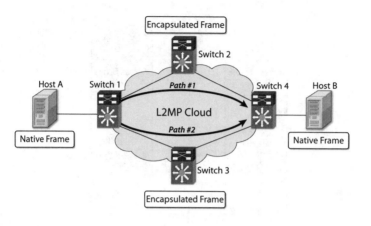

Figure 2-26   Known Unicast forwarding

Forwarding of Known Unicast Frames

D/RBridges use IS-IS to compute the shortest path between the ingress D/RBridge and the egress D/RBridge. If two or more paths have the same lower cost and Equal Cost Multi-Path (ECMP) is enabled, the traffic is spread among these paths using a hashing function that forwards all the frames of a given flow on the same path in order, to avoid frame reordering.

Figure 2-26 shows a frame traveling from Host A to Host B. It reaches SW1, that looks up the MAC address of Host B in its MAC forwarding table. The MAC address is found with the associated egress D/RBridge, in this case SW4. The frame is then encapsulated with the addition of the ingress/egress header, containing the ingress (SW1) and egress (SW4) D/RBridge addresses. While the frame propagates over the L2MP cloud, each D/RBridge checks the egress RBridge address to verify if the frame is for itself. If yes, it removes the additional header(s) and forwards the native Ethernet frame; otherwise it looks up the egress D/RBridge address and forwards the frame to the next D/RBridge. In this particular example, the frame may propagate either on Path #1 or on Path #2, since they are ECMPs.

Forwarding of Multidestination Frames

D/RBridges use IS-IS to compute one or more distribution trees where they forward multi-destination frames. The number of trees and the selection criteria vary between DBridges and RBridges, but the basic technique is the same. In the example of Figure 2-27, a single tree rooted in SW3 is computed.

When a D/RBridge receives a native multidestination Ethernet frame, it associates the frame with a distribution tree and encapsulates it with the ingress/egress header, where the ingress D/RBridge address and the distribution tree are contained. This differs slightly in DBridges and

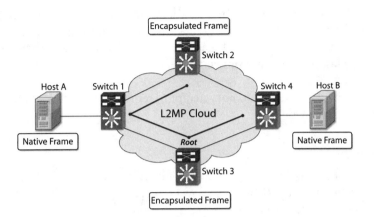

Figure 2-27 Multidestination Forwarding

RBridges. The egress D/RBridge is clearly not significant, since potentially the frame is for all the D/RBridges.

In the example of Figure 2-27, the frame arrives at SW1. SW1 encapsulates the frame and sends it to SW2 and SW3 on the only distribution tree available. SW3 forwards it to SW4.

To avoid temporary multicast loops during topology changes, D/RBridges perform a sanity check to make sure that a multidestination frame arrives on the expected link. In a nutshell, by using IS-IS, they compute the set of ingress D/RBridges that may source a frame on a given link, and they reject a frame if it comes from an ingress D/RBridge not belonging to the set. When a topology change occurs, D/RBridges recompute these sets.

In-Order Delivery

In-order delivery in L2MP networks may be violated for three main reasons:

1. **ECMP:** When multiple equal-cost paths exist, it is important to forward all the frames of a flow on the same path to preserve in-order delivery. Load balancing happens among flows, but if in-order delivery is desired, it must not happen inside a flow. All the D/RBridges have programmable hash functions that allow selecting the granularity of the load balancing and therefore guarantee in-order delivery, if desired.

2. **Going from unknown unicast to known unicast:** Unknown unicast frames are multi-destination frames that propagate over a distribution tree. When the unicast destination is learned (i.e., it becomes "known"), the frames become known unicast frames, and they start to propagate over the shortest path. A few frames may be reordered during this transition. This is pragmatically irrelevant, since a destination typically becomes known when it sends the first control traffic (e.g., ARP frame for IPv4 or FIP frames for FCoE) and well before it starts to send real data traffic.

3. **Topology changes:** The STP does not reorder frames during topology changes, but it can drop frames and, in general, it is much slower to converge. D/RBridges accept that topology changes are rare and that reordering a few frames is acceptable, however they provide fast topology convergence.

Both L2MP/MIM and L2MP/TRILL do not attempt to reorder frames and leave this task to the end station.

STP Compatibility

There has been a lot of discussion in the network community on how to deal with STP compatibility in a ECMP environment. D/RBridges allow connecting regular Ethernet clouds that use STP. Two models are possible: termination or participation.

In the termination model, the BPDUs (Bridge PDU) are simply discarded by a D/RBridge and are not propagated inside the L2MP. This potentially is a bit less efficient in detecting complex loops that involve, for instance, Ethernet hubs, but it is more future-oriented, since it allows eliminating STP on the backbone from day one.

The participation model requires D/RBridges to participate in the STP and to propagate the STP information over L2MP, with all the complexity involved in terminating multiple styles of STP.

Both DBridges and RBridges terminate the STP and do not propagate the BPDU over L2MP. This allows seamless interoperability with existing Ethernet switches (i.e., bridges).

End Station MAC Address Learning

IEEE 802.1 bridges learn MAC addresses by observing the source MAC address of data frames. D/RBridges use the same technique. In addition, they can also learn through IS-IS. This second method can be preferred in an environment where end stations authenticate themselves with the D/RBridges. In fact, it is through authentication that a D/RBridge is certain that a MAC address is legitimate and not spoofed, and therefore it can announce it through IS-IS, with a higher priority compared to an address learned by observing traffic.

VLANs

DBridges use the classical VLAN model, and they carry a single VID (VLAN ID) inside the frame. RBridges may use two VIDs: the inner VID, similar to the one DBridges use, and the outer VID, in the Next Hop Header, used by an encapsulated frame to traverse a legacy Ethernet cloud.

DBridges connect legacy Ethernet clouds either in a single point or with a technique similar to vPC (discussed in page 34), but Ethernet clouds remain at the periphery of L2MP.

RBridges support Ethernet clouds everywhere and therefore have more complexity in dealing with native Ethernet frames. In particular, for each VLAN on each Ethernet cloud, TRILL elects a particular RBridge to act as a VLAN forwarder. The VLAN forwarder is the only RBridge that can send and receive native Ethernet traffic for that VLAN.

The VLAN forwarder election process is convoluted, since it needs to detect possible inconsistent VLAN configurations, while minimizing the number of control messages used.

VLAN Pruning

All the forwarding information is computed independently of VLANs. This is also true for distribution trees. To avoid sending frames for a certain VLAN to a D/RBridge that has no ports on that VLAN, VLAN pruning is implemented by D/RBridges.

IGMP Snooping

IGMP snooping is a well-known technique implemented in almost all Ethernet switches to handle multicast traffic. Similarly, D/RBridges implement IGMP snooping at the edge of the L2MP cloud. IGMP frames are processed to determine interested receivers. Group membership information is advertised in the core of the L2MP cloud by using a dedicated control protocol. All D/RBridges compute outgoing interface lists based on this information.

Configuration

Historically, one of the big advantages of IEEE bridges has been the so-called plug-and-play (For example, they have a default configuration that automatically produces a working network, without requiring any management actions.) Over the years security concerns have grown and customers have started to prefer that switches ship with automatic configuration disabled. Manual configuration of switch IDs and other parameters has become the preferred way of operation of many network managers. D/RBridges support either a fully automated or a manual configuration.

Cisco DBridges

This section contains additional information about Cisco DBridges.

Frame Format

Figure 2-28 illustrates the frame format used by DBridges and in particular the ingress/egress header that is the only additional header used by DBridges.

The fields of the ingress/egress header are:

- ODA: 48 bits MAC address of the egress DBridge
- OSA: 48 bits MAC address of the ingress DBridge

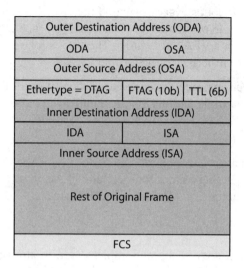

Figure 2-28   DBridge Frame Format

- Ethertype = DTAG: 16 bits Ethertype used to indicate that the frame has been encapsulated by a DBridge
- FTAG: 10 bits Forwarding Tag used to support multiple topologies
- TTL: 6 bits Time To Live

The fields that follow are the fields present in the native Ethernet frame, with the exception of the FCS that is recomputed to cover also the ingress/egress header.

Hierarchical MAC Addresses

Outer Destination Address (ODA) and Outer Source Address (OSA) are special MAC addresses assigned to DBridges. They have in the hierarchical structure shown in Figure 2-29.

The DBridge hierarchical MAC address format has the following fields:

- **U/L:** 1 bit Universal/Local. This field is defined in IEEE 802 and it is set to one to mean local MAC address administration.
- **I/G:** 1 bit Individual/Group. This field is defined in IEEE 802 and it is set to zero to address a single DBridge, or to one to address a group of DBridges.
- **Switch ID:** 12 bits. It is the unique identifier of a DBridge switch in a L2MP cloud. DBridges use a protocol to dynamically distribute switch IDs to each DBridge. Every DBridge has one or more Switch IDs.

Endnode ID [5:0]	U/L	I/G	Endnode ID [7:6]	Res	OOO /DL	Switch ID	SubSwitch ID	Local ID
6	1	1	2	1	1	12	8	16 bits

Figure 2-29   DBridge Hierarchical MAC Address Format

- **Subswitch ID:** 8 bits. It is a unique identifier used to address a switch in conjunction with an Emulated Switch (see page 50).

- **Local ID (LID):** 16 bits. It is the edge port identifier, signifying the port to which the host is attached. By making this the same as the port-ID, the forwarding decision at the destination DBridge is very simple. This field has significance local to the switch that assigns it. A DBridge can either send the frame to the correct edge-port, by using the LID in the ODA, without doing any additional MAC forwarding table lookups, or may choose to ignore this field and do an additional lookup to decide the egress port.

- **End Node ID:** 8 bits. It is used only in cases where the end station supports assignment of Hierarchical MAC addresses, via some protocol yet to be defined. Behind a single edge-port there could be many end stations, as in the case of server virtualization.

- **Out Of Order (OOO) in ODA:** 1 bit. It is used to specify that the frames can be spread across multiple paths independently of the hash function normally used for load balancing. Typically, frames belonging to the same flow are sent on the same path to avoid frame reordering. When this bit is set, this may no longer be true.

- **Don't Learn (DL) in OSA:** 1 bit. It is used to specify that learning of the association between the hierarchical MAC address and the classical MAC address must be disabled for frames with this bit set.

- **Res:** 1 bit. Reserved.

FTAG and Multitopology Support

The Forwarding TAG (FTAG) is a topology tag carried inside each frame. It is set by the ingress DBridge and honored by all subsequent DBridges, within that L2MP cloud. This is crucial to avoid loops due to inconsistent frame classification on different DBridges.

FTAG allows supporting multiple forwarding topologies. In existing Ethernet bridges, either each VLAN or a group of VLANs can have their own spanning tree instance and thus a specific forwarding topology for unicast traffic.

A similar mechanism is possible in DBridges with either a VLAN or a group of VLANs having their own instance of IS-IS identified by the FTAG, but this may not be the best approach, since L2MP achieves multipath inherently, independently of VLANs.

Instead, FTAG is particularly important to enable different forms of traffic engineering (different FTAGs for different class of users) and is a value-added feature of DBridges in comparison to RBridges.

For example, for multicast traffic it is possible to construct different multicast distribution trees and to use the FTAG to identify the tree over which a frame propagates.

In the future, the FTAG can be used to identify a forwarding topology based on other criteria such as protocol type, ingress port or some combination of L2/L3/L4 information.

Emulated Switch

The initial deployment of L2MP is for use in the core of Data Center networks, where bisectional bandwidth issues are of concern. At the periphery, classical Ethernet switches and hosts continue to exist, and they need to connect in a high available fashion to the L2MP backbone. The preferred way to connect them is via Etherchannel, exactly like in the cases of VSS and vPC.

To support an Etherchannel, two or more DBridges can host an Emulated Switch. The Emulated Switch is similar to vPC, but it is implemented using extensions to the L2MP protocols.

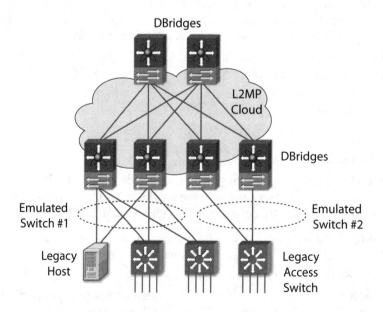

Figure 2-30   Emulated Switches

Figure 2-30 shows two pairs of DBridges hosting two Emulated Switches. The one on the right connects a single legacy Ethernet switch; the one on the left connects two legacy Ethernet switches and a host.

From an addressing perspective, each Emulated Switch has its own Switch ID; therefore in Figure 2-30 there are six Switch IDs assigned to the six DBridges and two Switch IDs assigned to the two Emulated Switches.

Each legacy switch or host inside the Emulated Switch is identified and addressed by a different subswitch ID, therefore Emulated Switch #1 has three subswitch IDs (two legacy access switches and one host) and the Emulated Switch #2 has a single subswitch ID.

Control plane protocols for the Emulated Switch are distributed across the DBridges that belong to the Emulated Switch and not located only on the Master. Data traffic is spread across both DBridges via ECMP (when received from other DBridges) and via Etherchannel (when received from legacy switches and hosts).

IETF RBridges and the TRILL Project

The IETF has a project named Transparent Interconnection of Lots of Links (TRILL) [18] for Layer 2 multipath and shortest-path frame forwarding in multihop IEEE 802.1-compliant Ethernet networks with arbitrary topologies, using IS-IS.

Frame Format

RBridges use the TRILL frame format shown in Figure 2-31.

Compared to the DBridge frame format of Figure 2-28, the RBridge frame format has an additional Next Hop Header.

NHDA (Next Hop Destination Address) is the MAC address of the next RBridge on the path and NHSA (Next Hop Source Address) is the MAC address of the RBridge sending the frame.

A classical VLAN is used to cross a legacy Ethernet cloud (Ethertype=CTAG, new IEEE 802.1 terminology for an IEEE 802.1Q VLAN).

In the TRILL header, RBridges are not addressed by MAC addresses, but by Nicknames (16 bits binary strings). Nicknames are nonhierarchical (this is a difference with DBridges) and are either manually assigned or automatically configured by IS-IS.

Few other fields are present in the TRILL header, namely:

- **V (Version):** 2-bit unsigned integer. TRILL Protocol Version. Current version is zero.
- **R (Reserved):** 2 bits.
- **M (Multidestination):** set to zero if the frame is a known unicast frame, set to one if it is a multidestination frame.

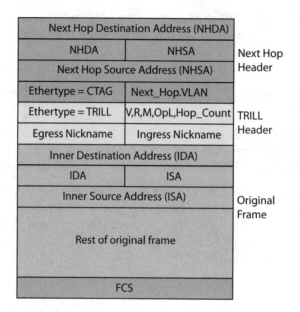

Figure 2-31   TRILL Frame Format

- **OpL (Options Length):** 5-bit unsigned integer. It indicates the presence of an optional option-header and it specifies its length in units of four octets.
- **Hop_Count:** 6-bit unsigned integer. Decremented by each RBridge that forwards the frame. The frame is discarded if Hop_Count reaches zero.

The FTAG field present in DBridges is missing. TRILL supports multitopology only for multicast, not for unicast. It accomplishes this by using a combination of the M bit and the egress Nickname. When the M bit is set, it indicates a multidestination frame, and therefore the egress Nickname is not used. In this case, TRILL stores the identification of the distribution tree in the egress Nickname by storing the Nickname of the root of the tree.

VEB: Virtual Ethernet Bridging

Long gone are the times when servers had a single CPU, a single Ethernet card (with a unique MAC address), and were running a single operating system. Today servers are much more complex. They have multiple CPU chips (i.e., sockets), each CPU chip contains multiple CPUs (i.e., cores), and each CPU is capable of running simultaneously one or more threads. These servers have significant I/O demands and they use multiple Ethernet NICs to connect to the network, to guarantee performance and high availability. These NICs are evolving to support SR-IOV (see page 54) and server virtualization.

Server Virtualization

Server virtualization is the only technique that allows using all the available cores without modifying/rewriting the applications. VMware ESX, Linux XEN, and Microsoft Hyper-V are well known virtualization solutions that allow running multiple Virtual Machines (VM) on a single server through the coordination of a hypervisor.

A VM is an instantiation of a logical server that behaves exactly as a standalone server, but it shares the hardware resources with the other VMs, in particular, for this discussion, the network resources.

The hypervisor implements inter-VM communication using a "software switch" module, among many other duties. This creates a different model compared to standalone servers.

Standalone servers connect to one or more Ethernet switches through dedicated switch ports (see Figure 2-32). Network policies applied to Ethernet switch ports (dashed line in Figure 2-32) are effectively applied to single standalone servers.

A logical server running in a VM connects to the software switch module in the hypervisor, and this in turn connects to one or more Ethernet switches (see Figure 2-33). Network policies applied to Ethernet switch ports (dashed line in Figure 2-33) are not very effective, since they are applied to all the VMs (i.e., logical servers) and cannot be specific to a single logical server.

Attempts to specify such policies in terms of source MAC addresses are also not particularly effective, since the MAC addresses used by the VMs are assigned by the virtualization software and may change over time. Moreover, this opens the system to MAC address spoofing attacks, in which, for example, a VM may try to use the MAC address of another VM.

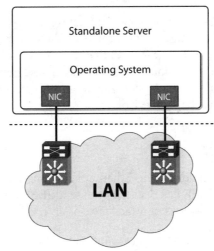

Figure 2-32 Standalone Server

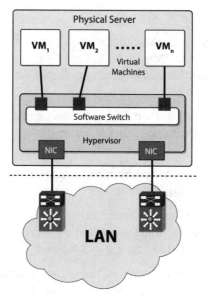

Figure 2-33   Logical Servers

Virtualization software also provides system administrators with the ability to move VMs on demand between different physical servers. This results in increased complexity in the management of network policies. The number of VMs tends to be much larger than the number of physical servers, and this creates scalability and manageability concerns.

SR-IOV

The Peripheral Component Interconnect - Special Interest Group (PCI-SIG) has a subgroup that produces specifications for NIC cards supporting I/O Virtualization (IOV). Of particular relevance is the area of Single Root IOV (SR-IOV) that deals with native I/O Virtualization in PCI Express topologies where there is a single root complex. These devices are designed to work in conjunction with server virtualization by allowing multiple VMs to natively share PCI Express devices, potentially bypassing the hypervisor.

The IEEE Standard Effort

IEEE has been in charge of standardizing Ethernet switching behavior since inception in the group IEEE 802.1. Recently IEEE has decided to extend IEEE 802.1 to also cover the Virtual Ethernet Bridges (VEB). Two avenues of attack are possible:

- Move the policies enforcement and the management inside the Ethernet adapter.
- Carry the VM identity to the Ethernet Switch.

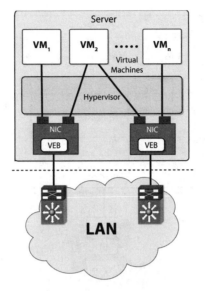

Figure 2-34   VEB in the Adapter

Cisco has also started to deliver a new architecture named VN-Link that contains products that are compliant with the IEEE effort.

VEB in the Adapter

When we use the term "VEB in the adapter," we refer to the fact that the adapter (NIC) is the place where the VEB is implemented (see Figure 2-34). This implies that large NIC manufacturers should start to integrate Ethernet switches, capable of enforcing policies, in their NICs.

At a first glance, this solution may look attractive, since it does not require changing the frame format on the wire between the NIC and the Ethernet switch; however, it has significant drawbacks. The NIC has to implement a complete Ethernet switch, with all the security components. This increases cost and complexity and subtracts valuable gates to other Upper Layer Protocol (ULP) features like TCP offload, RDMA, FC/SCSI, IPC queue pairs, and so on.

With the number of VMs increasing due to more powerful processors and to larger memories, there is also a potential scaling issue with respect to the number of VMs that can be supported, since each VM requires hardware resources in the NIC.

The management of a VEB in the adapter is also problematic. The IT engineers normally manage the servers, while the network is normally managed by a different group of network engineers. The VEB in the adapter requires that both groups coordinate to manage the servers, and this adds additional operational overhead.

To overcome these limitations the VEB in the switch architecture has been developed.

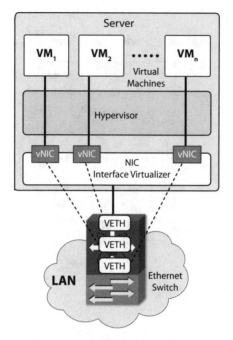

Figure 2-35 VEB in the Switch

VEB in the Switch

The "VEB in the switch" solution delegates complex and performance critical data path functions to an external Ethernet switch, as shown in Figure 2-35. The Ethernet switches are responsible of ensuring feature consistency to all the VMs, independently of where they are located (i.e., independently from which Hypervisor or physical server the logical server runs on).

The number of switches to be managed does not increase, since there are no switches inside the NICs. The need for the network managers to manage a server component is not present as well.

The NIC designers can use the available logical gates to provide better performance to ULPs, by improving data movement and ULP features like TCP offload, RDMA, and FC/SCSI.

This approach requires developing a new Ethernet tagging scheme between the NIC and the Ethernet switch to indicate the virtual NIC (vNIC) associated with the frame. Cisco has pioneered the Virtual NIC Tag (VNTag) scheme described in page 57. This is an Interface Virtualization (IV) scheme that moves the interfaces from the VMs to an external Ethernet switch and makes them virtual. This new virtual interfaces are called Virtual Ethernet (Veth) and the Ethernet switch operates on them as if they were physical ports. Whatever an Ethernet switch can do on a physical port it can do it on the Veth.

This new tag binds each vNIC to a Veth and vice versa. Policies are applied to Veths and therefore to vNICs. Policies may include Access Control Lists (ACLs), traffic management (for example, parameters for PFC and ETS), authentication, encryption, and so on.

This new tag is much more difficult to spoof than a MAC Address, since it is inserted by the NIC or the hypervisor and not by the VM.

When a VM moves from one server to another, its vNICs move with it, the Veths move with it, and the policies move with it. This guarantees feature and policy consistency independently of the location of the VM.

This approach requires a control protocol between the NIC and the Ethernet switch to consistently create, assign, modify, and terminate the relationship between vNICs and Veths. For example, when a VM moves from Host-A to Host-B, this control protocol is in charge of terminating the vNICs/Veths on the Ethernet switch where Host-A is connected, and of creating them on the Ethernet switch where Host-B is connected. The movement of the Veth also implies the consistent move of the associated policies.

Going back to Figure 2-35, the NIC contains an Interface Virtualizer (i.e., an entity that performs the frame dispatching to/from the vNICs). The Interface Virtualizer is not a switch. (For example, it does not allow the direct communication of two vNICs.) The Interface Virtualizer allows only one vNIC to communicate with the Ethernet switch and the Ethernet switch to communicate with one or more vNICs.

There is no change in the Ethernet switch model: The Ethernet switch just has an expanded number of ports (Veths), one for each connected vNIC. The Ethernet switch functionality for the virtual ports remains unchanged.

VNTag

The VNTag is an Ethernet tag that is inserted into the Ethernet frame immediately after the MAC-DA and MAC-SA pair (see Figure 2-36). The IEEE MACsec (authentication and encryption) tag may precede it.

VNTag is needed to augment the forwarding capability of an Ethernet switch and to make it capable to operate in a virtualized environment. In fact, a classical Ethernet switch does not forward a frame when the source and destination MAC address are on the same port, and therefore it is not capable of forwarding frames between two VMs connected on the same switch port. VNTag solves this and other issues by creating a virtual Ethernet interface per VM on the switch. Since the switch is capable of forwarding between these virtual Ethernet interfaces, it is capable of forwarding between VMs connected on the same physical port.

VNTag is a 6-bytes tag whose format is shown in Figure 2-37. The VNTag is used between the VEB in the Ethernet switch and the Interface Virtualizer. Its main concept is the "vif" (i.e., the virtual interface identifier). The vif appears in the VNTag as src_vif (source vif) and dst_vif (destination vif).

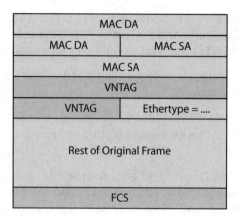

Figure 2-36 VNTag in an Ethernet Frame

The VNTag starts with two bytes of Ethertype = VNTag to identify this particular type of tag. The next four bytes have the following meaning:

- **v: version[2]:** Indicates the version of the VNTag protocol carried by this header, currently version zero.

- **r: reserved[1]:** This field is reserved for future use.

- **d: direction[1]:** d = 0 indicates that the frame is sourced from an Interface Virtualizer to the Ethernet switch. d = 1 indicates that the frame is sourced from the Ethernet switch to an Interface Virtualizer (one or more vNICs).

- **dst_vif[14] & p: pointer[1]:** These fields select the downlink interface(s) that receive a frame when sent from the Ethernet switch to the Interface Virtualizer. As such, they are meaningful when d = 1. When d = 0, these fields must be zero.

- **p = 0** indicates that dst_vif selects a single vNIC, typically used for unicast frames.

- **p = 1** indicates that dst_vif is an index into a virtual interface list table; this case is used for multicast frame delivery.

- **src_vif[12]:** Indicates the vNIC that sourced the frame. src_vif must be set appropriately for all frames from an Interface Virtualizer to the Ethernet switch (d = 0). In addition, src_vif may be set for frames headed toward the Interface Virtualizer (d = 1) as indicated by looped.

- **l: looped[1]:** Indicates that the Ethernet switch looped back the frame toward the Interface Virtualizer that originated it. In this situation, the Interface Virtualizer must ensure that the vNIC indicated by src_vif does not receive the frame, since it has originated the frame.

The vif is just an identifier of the association between a vNIC and a Veth on a given link. It has a meaning that is local to the link (physical port of the Ethernet switch), and it is not unique

Cisco Store - RTP
7100 Kit Creek Road
Morrisville, NC 27560
919-392-4020

Sales Receipt

Transaction #:   1396
Date: 7/15/2010   Time: 1:42:33 PM
Cashier: Andy   Register #:   1

Item   Description   Amount
==
158705888   Input Output Consolidat $32.00
            Discount   ($10.00)
400320   M & M's - Peanut $0.80
            Tax change code: No Tax

                    ================
            Sub Total $22.80
        RTP Sales Tax $1.77
              Total $24.57

        Cash Tendered $30.00
          Change Cash $5.43

You saved $10.00!

* 1 3 9 6 *
Thank you for shopping at
Cisco Store - RTP
We hope you'll come back soon!

dst_vif

d the Veth move. The existing association nated, and a new association is created on if that, being local to the new link, may be

in hardware by a VNTag-capable NIC or in

NICs in the server, but it can also be imple- plexer toward an Ethernet switch. This box

of an Interface Virtualizer and as such it hes. A Fabric Extender can also be seen as hernet multiplexer/demultiplexer. Its main out increasing the number of management all coast of the solution. The Nexus 2000 Fabric Extenders are also used in the Cisco

d to two Ethernet switches. The links that

ck Unit) box with 48 x 1GE ports toward switches. In this case, the Fabric Extender e VNTag on the 1GE ports.

ped together by using Etherchannel. In Extenders have the four uplinks grouped Fabric Extender has also the four uplinks grouped together into a single Etherchannel but connected in pairs to two separate Ethernet switches. This latter configuration requires that the two Ethernet switches are either part of a VSS, or they run vPC, or they are DBridges of a L2MP cloud (see page 38).

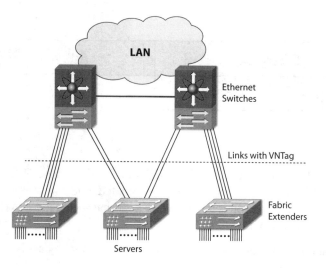

Figure 2-38 Fabric Extenders

A Nexus 5020, with a single point of management, can connect 12 Fabric Extender (4 x 10GE each, total 48 ports on the Nexus 5020) providing a total number of 576 x 1GE ports, in 12 RUs. In fact the Fabric extenders are not individually managed, only the Nexus 5000 is.

Another example is a Fabric Extender with 32 x 10GE ports toward the servers and 8 x 10GE ports toward the Ethernet switches. In this case, the Fabric Extender uses 256 vifs and dynamically assigns them to the 32 x 10GE ports that also use VNTag toward the server. This illustrates the possibility to aggregate links that already use VNTag.

Five of these Fabric Extenders, in association with a Nexus 5020, can provide 160 x 10GE ports, with Unified Fabric support, in 7 RUs, with a single point of management.

The Fabric Extenders can be located very close to the servers and cheap copper connections can be used between the servers and the Fabric Extenders. The Ethernet switches can be located at the end-of-row and more expensive fiber connections used between the fabric extenders and the Ethernet switches. The resulting solution is oversubscribed but provides 10GE connectivity at low cost and with a reduced number of management points.

VN-Link

The Virtual Network Link (VN-Link) was collaboratively developed by Cisco and VMware to cover the issues of the VEBs and more. VN-Link simplifies the management and administration of a virtualized environment by bringing the servers and the networks closer. VN-Link delivers networkwide VM visibility and mobility with consistent policy management.

As part of the development of VN-Link, a specification has been submitted to IEEE 802.1 to support network interface virtualization on hardware-based networking platforms through VEB in the switch.

VN-Link and the Nexus 1000V

The Nexus 1000V is the first implementation of the VN-link architecture. It is a Cisco software switch embedded into VMware ESX hypervisor. It is compliant with the VMware virtual Network Distributed Switch (vNDS) API that was jointly developed by Cisco and VMware. VM policy enforcement is applied to and migrated with the VM when a VMotion or Distributed Resource Scheduler (DRS) moves a VM. Not only the policies are moved with the VM, but also all the statistical counters, the Netflow status and ERSPAN sessions.

Network Policies are called Port Profiles and are created by the network administrator on the Nexus 1000V using, for example, CLI commands. Port Profiles are automatically populated inside VMware Virtual Center (VC). Port Profiles are visible inside VMware Virtual Infrastructure Client as Port Groups and the server administrator can assign them to vNICs and therefore ultimately to VMs.

Port Profiles are the constructs in VN-Link that truly enable a collaborative operational model between the server administrator and the network administrator without requiring them to use any new management tool.

Veths and Port Profiles are the basic building blocks to enable automated VM connectivity as well as mobility of policies (i.e., to allow the interface configuration, interface state, and interface statistics to move with a virtual machine from server to server). This also guarantees that security and connectivity policies are persistent.

Nexus 1000V is a member of the Nexus family of switches, and it runs NX-OS. Figure 2-39 shows the basic components of the Nexus 1000V. The "Nexus 1000V VEM" (Virtual Ethernet Module) is installed in VMware ESXs and remotely configured and managed by the Nexus 1000V Virtual Supervisor Module (VSM) that runs in an NX-OS appliance (virtual or physical) or in a Nexus family switch, like the Nexus 5000 or the Nexus 7000. The dashed lines in Figure 2-39 indicate the management and configuration relationship between the VEMs and VSM. A VSM can manage multiple VEMs. In addition, a VSM maintains the VMware Virtual Center provisioning model for server administration.

Being part of the Nexus family, the Nexus 1000V provides many value added features over a regular software switch, such as ACLs, QoS marking and queueing, Cisco TrustSec, CDP v2, Netflow V9, Port Profiles, Cisco CLI, XMP API, SNMP Read/Write, detailed interface counters & statistics, Port Security, and so on. For example, it supports Encapsulated Remote SPAN (ERSPAN) to mirror the traffic of a VM to an external sniffer located centrally in the data center and also during the movement of the VM.

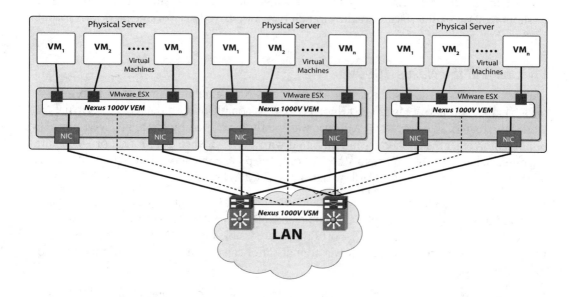

Figure 2-39   Nexus 1000V

VN-Link and the Nexus 5000

The Nexus 5000 supports the VN-Link architecture. It operates as a VEB in the switch (see page 56) using VNTag (see page 57) between the Interface Virtualizer in the hypervisor and the Nexus 5000.

The Interface Virtualizer is in charge of tagging the frames leaving the VM and this can happen in two ways:

- The first approach is to apply VNTag in software in the hypervisor switch (either the Nexus 1000V or the VMware switch) and then forward the packet to the Nexus 5000.
- The second approach is to have a NIC (e.g., an SR-IOV NIC) that is capable of adding VNTag in hardware. In this second approach, a capable SR-IOV NIC can also implement hypervisor bypass.

The external behavior and the benefits are the same of using VN-Link on the Nexus 1000V, but here all the Ethernet features (switching, ACLs, ERSPAN, QoS, and so on) are performed completely in hardware at wire rate by the Nexus 5000.

Network Policies are still defined in terms of Port Profiles, and VMotion/DRS is supported as in the previous case as well as all the other VN-Link features.

Questions and Answers

Does FCoE Uses Credits?

Q: Is the FC buffer-to-buffer credits mechanism needed/available for FCoE to manage queueing capacity?

A: In the lossless Ethernet required by FCoE, the FC buffer-to-buffer credits mechanism is replaced by the Priority-based Flow Control (or Per Priority Pause, see page 20).

High Availability of PAUSE and Credits

Q: Are there any "high availability" differences between PAUSE and credits?

A: There is no appreciable difference between the high availability of PAUSE or credits. If a switch fails, all the frames that are temporarily stored in the switch are lost, independently of credits or PAUSE. If a credit or PAUSE is lost, they are recovered, even if in different ways: Credits have a credit recovery scheme, PAUSE is soft-state, and it is just retransmitted.

Queue Size

Q: Is there any concern about the amount of queuing that would occur if the switches need to be paused for a long period?

A: The amount of queueing required by PAUSE is related to the link speed and the propagation delay. The propagation delay in Data Centers is typically very low.

PAUSE implementations typically require one round-trip delay of buffers, plus three MTUs.

The speed of light over copper or fiber optics is 200 meters/microsecond; one kilometer requires 5 microseconds one-way and 10 microseconds round-trip.

For 1 Km, single round-trips require 10 microseconds. At 10 Gbit/s, 10,000 bits are sent in one microsecond (i.e., the memory required to store one round-trip is 100,000 bits [12.5 KB], plus 3 MTUs [each 9 KB] for a total of 29.5 KB).

For 10Km it is 125 KB + 27 KB = 152 KB.

Long-Haul

Q: Can Lossless Ethernet be applied to achieve long-haul cross-site connectivity between Data Centers? For example using optical DWDM with 10GE ports between two sites?

A: There are three limiting factors to the distance between two data centers: optics availability, buffer size, and error rate:

- **Optics:** Of course there is the need to have optics that can cover the required distance and a DWDM equipment that is compatible with the optics used on the lossless switches.

- **Buffer size:** We discussed buffer size in page 63. To support PAUSE between two data centers geographically separated, the amount of buffers need to increase in a similar fashion to the number of credits required by Fibre Channel. At 100 Km the buffers requirement is 1.3 MB.

- **Error Rate:** The error rate needs to stay low for protocols like FCoE (see page 67) to continue to work. An error rate of 10^{-15} (approximately one bit error in a day) or better is desirable.

FECN/BECN

Q: Is PFC similar to FECN/BECN?

A: No, PFC is similar to VC_RDY in Fibre Channel. The equivalent of FECN/BECN is QCN (see page 25).

Configuration

Q: Is the PFC queue selection handled/configured on the 10GE adapter side or on the switch side or on both?

A: Maintaining a consistent configuration is key to obtain a consistent behavior. This task is delegated to the DCBX protocol, see page 22.

Bandwidth Prioritization

Q: High Definition video conferencing has used QoS to prioritize bandwidth in H.323 networks; will the FCoE bandwidth manager allow this UDP video to be lossless?

A: Lossless Ethernet (see page 15) and Enhanced Transmission Selection (see page 23) can be used by any application and are not restricted to FCoE. Practically, it depends on the application how to take advantage of them. In general, traffic like NFS, iSCSI, VoIP would all be able to gain benefits from an underlying lossless transport.

Storage Bandwidth

Q: How much of a 10GE link is available for Fiber Channel traffic with FCoE?

A: The amount of bandwidth available for Fibre Channel over a Unified Fabric connection depends from the capability of the NIC (more appropriately CNA, see page 74) and on the parameters programmed in Enhanced Transmission Selection (see page 23).

Fibre Channel bandwidth is computed at the physical layer, while Ethernet bandwidth is computed at the data link layer, therefore 4GFC corresponds to 3.4 Gbit/s of Ethernet speed and 8GFC corresponds to 6.8 Gbit/s of Ethernet speed. This creates the paradox that a 10GE link is roughly equivalent to a hypothetical 12GFC link!

Initial CNAs were able to carry over a 10GE link the equivalent of a 4GFC or of a 8GFC bandwidth of Fibre Channel traffic. Most of current CNAs can use all the bandwidth of a 10GE link to carry FC traffic.

Cisco DCB/FCoE Support

Q: What Cisco Switch hardware will support DCB/FCoE? Only the Nexus switches or also other platforms, for example the Catalyst 6500?

A: At the time of writing (June 2009) the Nexus switches (Nexus 5000 and 7000) are currently the only platforms that have the internal design capable of operating lossless, and they will support these capabilities. The Nexus 5000 has these capabilities shipping today; the Nexus 7000 will have them in the near future.

10GE NICs

Q: To support DCB/FCoE, is 10GE needed end-to-end? For example, CPU to storage device?

A: The speeds of the link is variable from 1 to 10 Gbit/s in initial deployments, but starting in 2009 it is expected that the adoption of 10GE end-to-end will start to increase, with 40GE starting to appear in the second half of 2010 and 100GE one year later, mostly for backbone applications. 10GE deployments will be initially in the servers, with storage array targets arriving approximately one year later.

IP Routing

Q: Is the interface to the IP routed world handled by Nexus switches only or is any router capable of interfacing lossless Ethernet?

A: Lossless Ethernet is an extension of Ethernet developed in the IEEE 802.1 standards body. Any router with the proper interfaces is capable of routing IP frames from and to lossless Ethernet networks.

Lossless Ethernet Versus Infiniband

Q: How does Lossless Ethernet compete with 12x Infiniband? For example, in terms of bandwidth?

A: 10GE is less than 12x IB, but Ethernet has a roadmap to 40GE and 100GE. The big question is how important is bandwidth versus the ability to support a converged network model. IB has capabilities very specific to low latency computing applications, and due to this and the additional management skill sets required to install and manage it, IB is only installed in specific corner cases.

Nomenclature

The Ethernet extensions discussed in this chapter are grouped under different names.

Data Center Bridging (DCB) refers to the standardization activities in IEEE 802.1. Projects under development in the IEEE 802.1 DCB task group are

- Priority-based Flow Control (see [6])
- Bandwidth Management (see [7])
- Configuration (DCBX) (see [7])
- Congestion Notification (see [8])

DCB specifications submitted to IEEE, but not standard, are also called DCB v0 (version zero) and several vendors, to introduce products in a timely fashion, claim compatibility with DCB v0.

The terms Converged Enhanced Ethernet (CEE) and Data Center Ethernet (DCE) have also been used to group these techniques under common umbrellas.

Chapter 3

Fibre Channel over Ethernet

Introduction

Fibre Channel over Ethernet (FCoE) is a standard that has been developed by the FC-BB-5 working group of INCITS Technical Committee T11 [13], [14], [15], [17]. FCoE is based on the observation that Fibre Channel is the dominant storage protocol in the Data Center and that any viable I/O consolidation solution for storage must be based on the Fibre Channel model.

The idea behind FCoE is extremely simple: implement I/O consolidation by carrying each Fibre Channel frame inside an Ethernet frame. SCSI is mapped over FC as in native Fibre Channel and each resulting FC frame is encapsulated in an Ethernet frame. The encapsulation is performed on a frame-by-frame basis; therefore, it is completely stateless and does not require fragmentation nor reassembly.

Figure 3-1 shows an example of I/O consolidation using FCoE in which the only connectivity needed on the server is Ethernet, while separate backbones are still maintained for LAN and SAN. FCoE allows Fibre Channel traffic to share Ethernet links with other traffic, as shown in Figure 3-2.

From a Fibre Channel standpoint, in a sense FCoE defines a new form of connectivity over a new type of cable called Ethernet network. From an Ethernet standpoint FCoE is yet another Upper Layer Protocol (ULP) to be transported in parallel to IPv4, IPv6, and so on (see Figure 3-3).

FCoE poses some requirements on the underlying Ethernet network, the most important one being lossless. Lossless can be simply achieved by the PAUSE mechanism (see page 15). More realistically, in an I/O consolidation environment, PFC is used (see page 20) and additional protocols like DCBX (see page 22) facilitate deployment. FCoE also requires support of jumbo frames, since FC frames are not fragmented (see page 80).

This chapter introduces Fibre Channel and explains the protocol organization and the usage models of FCoE.

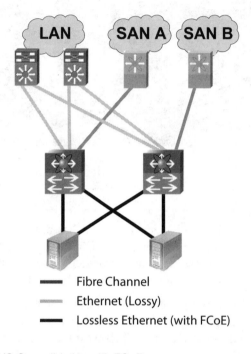

Figure 3-1   Example of I/O Consolidation with FCoE

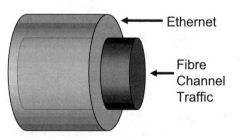

Figure 3-2   FCoE Link Sharing

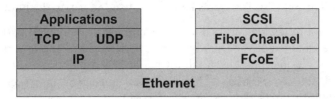

Figure 3-3 ULPs over Ethernet

Fibre Channel

Fibre Channel is the preeminent technology used today for storage networking. Among the technological reasons for its success, we can list:

- Native support to map SCSI operations over Fibre Channel protocol structures (the Exchange construct, see [11])
- Native protocol support for large data transfers (the Sequence construct, see [11])
- Simplified implementations due to the lossless behavior of Fibre Channel fabrics

Figure 3-4 shows the Fibre Channel frame format.

SOF		
R_CTL	D_ID	
CS_CTL	S_ID	
Type	F_CTL	
SEQ_ID	DF_CTL	SEQ_CNT
OX_ID		RX_ID
Parameter		
Data Field		
FC-CRC		
EOF		

Figure 3-4 Fibre Channel Frame Format

The Start of Frame (SOF) and End of Frame (EOF) are special FC transmission words that act as frame delimiters. The FC-CRC is 4 bytes long and is used to verify the integrity of the frame.

The FC header is 24 bytes long and contains several fields associated with the identification and control of the Data Field. The Data Field is of variable size, ranging from 0 to 2112 bytes. The fields of the FC header provide to Fibre Channel the semantic to natively map SCSI. For example, a large data transfer is natively handled as a Sequence of frames related by the value of the Sequence_ID (SEQ_ID) field of the FC Header. Multiple Sequences may be related together as belonging to the same FC Exchange. FC frames belonging to the same Exchange are related by the value of the OX_ID and RX_ID fields in the FC Header. An Exchange is the FC protocol construct that natively maps a SCSI operation.

Fibre Channel devices are called Nodes in standards. Each Node has one or more physical ports that connect to the ports of other devices.

Fibre Channel is a layered architecture defined by five different functional levels, named FC-0 through FC-4:

- The FC-0 level defines the functions of transmission and reception over specific physical media.
- The FC-1 level defines the transmission protocol, including serial encoding, decoding, and error control.
- The FC-2 level defines the Fibre Channel framing (e.g., the frame format), the transport services, and the control functions necessary for information transfer.
- The FC-3 level defines optional services common across multiple ports of a node.
- The FC-4 level defines the mappings supporting Upper Level Protocols, such as SCSI, IPv4, or IPv6.

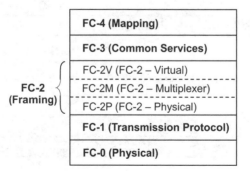

Figure 3-5 Fibre Channel Levels and Sublevels

To provide better support for virtualization, the FC-2 level is split in three sublevels:

- FC-2P (FC-2 – Physical), defining the buffer-to-buffer flow control function for a specific physical port
- FC-2M (FC-2 – Multiplexer), defining the multiplexing of Fibre Channel frames from instances of the FC-2P sublevel to instances of the FC-2V sublevel
- FC-2V (FC-2 – Virtual), defining how to handle Fibre Channel frames to support higher levels.

Figure 3-5 shows the functional levels of the Fibre Channel architecture. Knowing the Fibre Channel layering allows a proper understanding of FCoE.

Fibre Channel Architectural Models

Figure 3-6 shows the relationship between physical ports and functional levels in a Fibre Channel end device (i.e., a Node), commercially known as HBA. This section is generic for Fibre Channel and not specific on FCoE.

Each physical port of a Fibre Channel Node is called Physical N_Port (PN_Port). A PN_Port is an instance of the FC-0 and FC-1 levels and of the FC-2P sublevel. An instance of the FC-2V sublevel is called Virtual N_Port (VN_Port), and an instance of the FC-2M sublevel is called Multiplexer. A Fibre Channel Node supports multiple VN_Ports and multiple PN_Ports. The Multiplexer is the architectural entity multiplexing Fibre Channel frames between PN_Ports and VN_Ports. Each VN_Port supports the FC-3 and FC-4 levels.

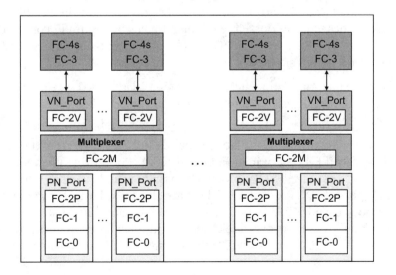

Figure 3-6 FC Node Model

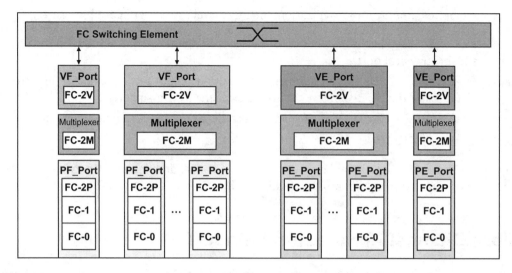

Figure 3-7   FC Switch Model

Figure 3-7 shows the relationship between physical ports and functional levels in a Fibre Channel Switch. This model encompasses both Fibre Channel directors and fabric switches.

Each physical port of a Fibre Channel Switch is called Physical F_Port (PF_Port) if connected to a Node port (i.e., a PN_Port) or Physical E_Port (PE_Port) if connected to another Switch port (i.e., another PE_Port). A PF_Port or PE_Port is an instance of the FC-0 and FC-1 levels and of the FC-2P sublevel. A PF_Port may support multiple instances of the FC-2V sublevel, each called Virtual F_Port (VF_Port). A PE_Port may support multiple instances of the FC-2V sublevel, each called Virtual E_Port (VE_Port). Multiplexers (i.e., instances of the FC-2M sublevel) are the architectural entities multiplexing Fibre Channel frames between PF_Ports and VF_Ports and between PE_Ports and PE_Ports. The FC Switching Element is the architectural entity forwarding Fibre Channel frames among VF_Ports and VE_Ports.

Fibre Channel uses unique nonvolatile names, called Name_Identifiers [11] to identify Fibre Channel entities. Each VN_Port acquires a 24-bit address identifier, called N_Port_ID, to perform communications. Name_Identifiers and N_Port_IDs are also known as WWNs and FC_IDs.

The first VN_Port connecting to an FC fabric acquires an N_Port_ID from the fabric by performing a process called Fabric Login or FLOGI. The VF_Port at the other end of the Fibre Channel link participates in the FLOGI process by assigning an N_Port_ID to the requesting VN_Port. The additional VN_Ports of a PN_Port acquire an N_Port_ID through a variant of the FLOGI protocol, called NPIV FDISC. This algorithm results in a particular association between VN_Ports and VF_Ports over an FC link: within each fabric there is a single VF_Port associated with the set of VN_Ports of a PN_Port. This relationship is shown in Figure 3-8.

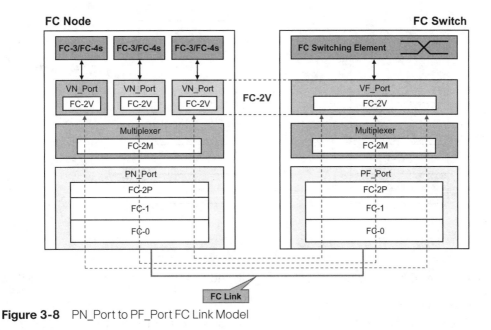

Figure 3-8 PN_Port to PF_Port FC Link Model

FCoE Mapping

FCoE maps the FC-2V sublevel of Fibre Channel over Ethernet, leveraging Ethernet extensions to achieve the same lossless service that native Fibre Channel links provide. Keeping the FC-2V sublevel and the above levels unchanged means that FCoE is transparent to the operating systems. This means that customers can maintain the same operational and management models of Fibre Channel. The FCoE mapping is shown in Figure 3-9. The credit-based flow control of the Fibre Channel FC-2P sublevel is replaced by Pause-based flow control or by Priority-based flow control in FCoE.

An alternative way to look at the FCoE mapping is to see FCoE as defining a new type of Fibre Channel link, an Ethernet network. This allows understanding the fundamental difference between native Fibre Channel and FCoE: A native Fibre Channel link is a point-to-point link, while a Ethernet network is inherently multi-access, even if composed only by full duplex links. FCoE relies on an auxiliary control protocol, FCoE Initialization Protocol (FIP), to reduce a multi-access Ethernet network to a set of point-to-point Virtual Links for FCoE use. In this way FCoE can continue to operate according to the FC model of operation. FCoE and FIP

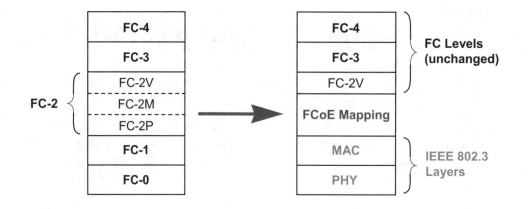

Figure 3-9   FCoE Mapping

have two different Ethertypes (i.e., 8906h for FCoE and 8914h for FIP) and may be classified as follows:

- FCoE is the data plane protocol. It is used to carry most of the FC frames and all the SCSI traffic. It is a data intensive protocol and typically it is switched in hardware.
- FIP is the control plane protocol. It is used to discover the FCoE entities connected to an Ethernet network and to establish and maintain Virtual Links for FCoE. It is not a data intensive protocol and typically it is implemented in software on the switch supervisor processor.

FCoE Architectural Models

In FCoE the architectural entity corresponding to an FC Node is called FCoE Node or ENode. An ENode is a Fibre Channel HBA implemented within an Ethernet NIC, commercially known as Converged Network Adapter (CNA).

The architectural entity corresponding to an FC Switch is called FCoE Forwarder or FCF, commercially known as FCoE switch.

ENodes and FCFs communicate through Ethernet ports supporting lossless Ethernet MACs. FCoE Virtual Links replace the physical Fibre Channel links by encapsulating FC frames in Ethernet frames. An FCoE Virtual Link is identified by the pair of MAC addresses of the two link end-points. FCoE supports VN_Port to VF_Port Virtual Links and VE_Port to VE_Port Virtual Links.

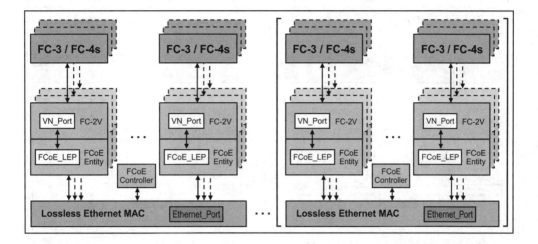

Figure 3-10 ENode Architectural Model

Figure 3-10 shows the functional model of an ENode, where the bracketed functional components are optional. An ENode is functionally composed of at least one lossless Ethernet MAC coupled with an FCoE Controller function.

The FCoE Controller is the functional entity processing the FIP protocol and instantiating VN_Ports and FCoE_LEPs (FCoE Link End-Points) as needed. The FCoE_LEP is the functional entity performing the encapsulation of FC frames into FCoE frames in transmission and the decapsulation of FCoE frames into FC frames in reception. Each VN_Port is paired with one FCoE_LEP.

For an ENode, the FCoE Controller

■ Discovers over which VLANs FCoE services are available

■ In these VLANs initiates the FIP Discovery protocol to discover VF_Port capable FCF-MACs connected to the same lossless Ethernet network

■ Initiates FIP FLOGI Exchanges and instantiates a VN_Port/FCoE_LEP pair for any successful completion of a FIP FLOGI Exchange

■ Initiates FIP NPIV FDISC Exchanges and instantiates a VN_Port/FCoE_LEP pair for any successful completion of a FIP NPIV FDISC Exchange

■ De-instantiates a VN_Port/FCoE_LEP pair when that VN_Port is logged out

■ Maintains the state of the VN_Port to VF_Port Virtual Links by monitoring received FIP Discovery Advertisement messages and by generating appropriate FIP Keep Alive messages

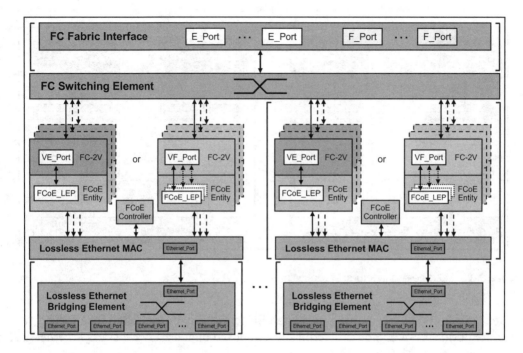

Figure 3-11   FCF Architectural Model

Figure 3-11 shows the functional model of an FCF, where the bracketed functional components are optional.

An FCF is functionally composed of a Fibre Channel Switching Element with at least one lossless Ethernet MAC (FCF-MAC). Each FCF-MAC is coupled with an FCoE Controller function. Each FCF-MAC may be coupled with a Losseless Ethernet bridging element. The Fibre Channel Switching Element may be coupled with a Fibre Channel Fabric interface, providing native E_Port and F_Port connectivity. An FCF forwards FCoE frames addressed to one of its FCF-MACs based on the D_ID of the encapsulated FC frames.

An FCF-MAC supports the instantiation of VE_Ports or VF_Ports. An FCF-MAC supporting the instantiation of VE_Ports is referred to as a VE_Port capable FCF-MAC. An FCF-MAC supporting the instantiation of VF_Ports is referred to as a VF_Port capable FCF-MAC. Each VF_Port is paired with one or more FCoE_LEPs. Each VE_Port is paired with one FCoE_LEP.

For a VF_Port capable FCF-MAC, the FCoE Controller

- Participates to the FIP VLAN Discovery protocol initiated by ENodes
- Participates to the FIP Discovery protocol initiated by ENodes

- Instantiates a VF_Port and an FCoE_LEP for any successful completion of a FIP FLOGI Exchange initiated by an ENode

- Instantiates an additional FCoE_LEP for any successful completion of a FIP NPIV FDISC Exchange initiated by an already logged in ENode

- When a VN_Port is logged out, de-instantiates the FCoE_LEP associated to that VN_Port and the corresponding VF_Port if that FCoE_LEP was the only one associated with that VF_Port

- Maintains the state of the VN_Port to VF_Port Virtual Links by monitoring received FIP Keep Alive messages and by generating appropriate FIP Discovery Advertisement messages

For a VE_Port capable FCF-MAC, the FCoE Controller

- Performs the FIP VLAN Discovery protocol

- Performs the FIP Discovery protocol

- Instantiates a VE_Port and a FCoE_LEP for any successful completion of a FIP ELP Exchange (the FCoE equivalent of a switch to switch link exchange in Fibre Channel)

- Maintains the state of the VE_Port to VE_Port virtual links by monitoring received FIP Discovery Advertisement messages and by generating them

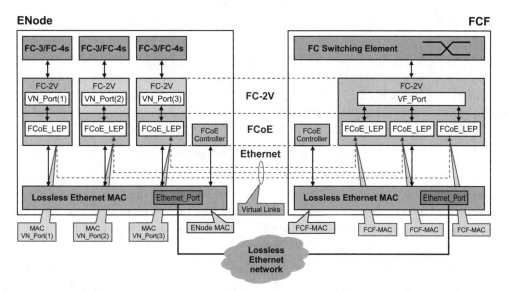

Figure 3-12   VN_Port to VF_Port Virtual Links

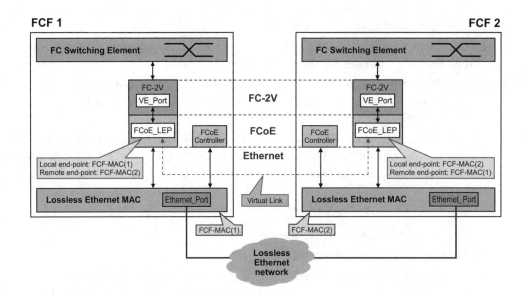

Figure 3-13   VE_Port to VE_Port Virtual Link

Figure 3-12 shows the relationship between VN_Ports and VF_Ports in an FCoE environment. In particular, Figure 3-12 shows the FCoE Virtual Links connecting the FCoE_LEPs of the VN_Ports with the FCoE_LEPs of the VF_Port, and the MAC addresses defining these Virtual Links.

It is interesting to correlate Figure 3-12 with Figure 3-8. The relationships among the entities at the FC-2V sublevel of Fibre Channel are equal in the two figures. This is in accordance with the mapping defined in Figure 3-9 and explains why FCoE allows a seamless integration with existing Fibre Channel: The lower layers are different, but the upper layers, where the interface with Operating Systems and management tools are located, are the same.

Figure 3-13 shows the relationship between VE_Ports in an FCoE environment.

Different vendors may choose to implement an FCF in different ways. The main difference is the presence (or absence) of one or more Ethernet bridges inside the FCF, as allowed by the model of Figure 3-11. Below each Lossless Ethernet MAC there is an optional Lossless Ethernet Bridging Element. This is not strictly needed for FCoE, but it is of paramount importance to provide a global I/O consolidation solution.

The FCF architecture is a good match for the general architecture of a multiprotocol router and therefore it is easy to foresee that the FCF functionality may be added to a multiprotocol router (see page 118).

FCoE Benefits

The FCoE benefits are similar to those of other I/O consolidation solutions. For example, fewer cables are needed, both block I/O & Ethernet traffic can co-exist on the same cable, fewer adapters are needed, and less power is required.

To these generic benefits, FCoE adds the additional advantage of being completely part of the Fibre Channel architecture (i.e., seamless integration with existing FC SANs, reuse of existing FC SAN tools, and management constructs).

Another important advantage is that FCoE requires no gateways. In fact the encapsulation/decapsulation functions simply add or remove an Ethernet envelope around an FC frame: The FC frame is untouched and the operation is completely stateless. This is shown in Figure 3-14.

In FC fabrics, zoning is a basic provisioning function that is used by storage administrators to give hosts access to storage. FCFs continue to offer an unmodified zoning function, ensuring that FC storage allocation and security mechanisms are unaffected.

The same consideration applies to other Fibre Channel services, for example:

- **distributed Name Server (dNS):** The dNS is an FC distributed naming database that also applies to FCoE-based SANs.

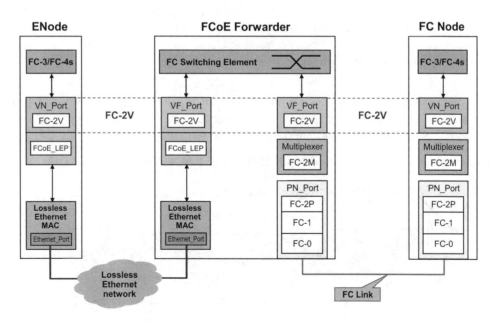

Figure 3-14   Gateway-Less FCoE

- **Registered State Change Notification (RSCN):** This FC notification functionality is fully supported on FCoE and FCoE adapters receive RSCNs as FC HBAs.
- **Fibre Channel Shortest Path First (FSPF):** FSPF is the FC routing protocol and is used to compute FC forwarding in a mixed FC/FCoE environment.

An FCoE-connected server is just a SCSI initiator over FC, exactly as if the server were connected over native FC (see page 108). The same applies to FCoE-connected storage arrays: they are just SCSI targets over FC. The management tools that customers use to manage and maintain their SANs today can be used in an FCoE environment.

Services utilizing storage virtualization or server virtualization continue to work with FCoE, since everything from the FC-2V sublevel upward remains the same.

FCoE Data Plane

The FCoE encapsulation is shown in Figure 3-15.

Starting from the inside out, there is the FC Payload that can be up to 2112 bytes. Most implementations use 2 KB Payloads, hence the pragmatic requirement to support Ethernet jumbo frames. The FC Payload is wrapped in an FC frame that contains an unmodified FC header and the CRC. Next is the FCoE header and trailer that contain the encoded FC Start of Frame (SOF) and End of Frame (EOF). In native FC SOF and EOF are ordered sets that contain code violations, and therefore they need to be re-encoded in FCoE. Finally, there is the Ethernet header that contains Ethertype = FCoE and the Ethernet trailer that contains the FCS (Frame Check Sequence).

Figure 3-16 shows the field sizes: The maximum size of an FCoE frame is 2180 bytes. To provide some margin for growth, FCoE recommends that the Ethernet infrastructure support jumbo frames up to 2.5 KB (baby jumbo frames). Every Cisco switch supports baby jumbo frames.

Figure 3-17 shows a detailed view of an Ethernet frame that includes an FCoE PDU.

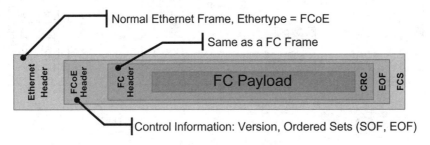

Figure 3-15   FCoE Encapsulation

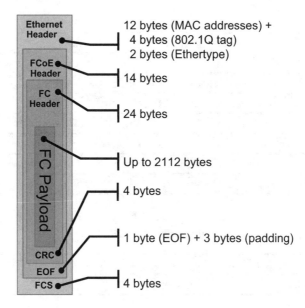

12 bytes (MAC addresses) +
 4 bytes (802.1Q tag)
 2 bytes (Ethertype)

14 bytes

24 bytes

Up to 2112 bytes

4 bytes

1 byte (EOF) + 3 bytes (padding)

4 bytes

Figure 3-16 FCoE Frame Size

The first 48-bits in the frame are used to specify the Destination MAC address, and the next 48-bits specify the Source MAC Addresses. The 32-bit IEEE 802.1Q Tag provides the same function as it does for Virtual LANs, allowing multiple virtual networks across a single physical infrastructure. It also includes the Priority field that must be present to be able to deploy PFC (see page 20).

FCoE has its own Ethertype (i.e., 8906h) as designated by the next 16 bits, followed by the 4-bit FCoE version field. The next 100-bits are reserved and have been inserted so that, even in the presence of minimum size FC frames, the Ethernet payload is greater or equal to 46 bytes, thus avoiding the need to pad the Ethernet payload. In fact, FCoE frames are never padded.

The 8-bit Start of Frame (SOF) follows and it is encoded as in FCIP [12]. The next field is the actual FC frame including the FC CRC, followed by the 8-bit End of Frame (EOF) delimiter, again encoded as in FCIP [12].

The EOF is followed by 24 reserved bits and the frame ends with the final 32-bits dedicated to the Ethernet FCS.

The FC header is maintained unmodified so that when a traditional FC SAN is connected to an FCoE-capable switch, the frame is easily encapsulated and decapsulated. This capability enables FCoE to integrate with existing FC SANs without the need of a gateway.

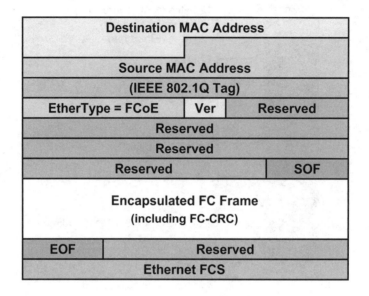

Figure 3-17   FCoE Frame Format

FCoE Topologies

FCoE can be deployed in a variety of topologies, depending on the business needs of a company and the products chosen. Figure 3-18 depicts a simple FCoE topology where I/O consolidation is achieved at the access layer of the network.

In the scenario depicted in Figure 3-18, FCoE is used to consolidate traffic from discrete servers to FCoE enabled switches. The servers contain the ENodes (CNA) that implement the VN_Ports, while the FCoE switches (FCFs) implement the VF_Ports.

The FCoE switches pass FC traffic to the attached FC SANs and Ethernet traffic to the attached LAN. This deployment model provides the greatest value for a customer that has a large installed base of LAN and SAN environments, since it allows a phased approach to I/O consolidation.

Figure 3-19 shows a similar approach for blade server deployments, where the only switching element that needs to be present inside the blade server is a lossless Ethernet Bridge. The CNAs on the Server Blades implement the VN_Ports, while the FCoE switches implement the VF_Ports. The Lossless Bridges inside the Blade Server do not need to be FCoE-aware, since they act purely at the Ethernet layer.

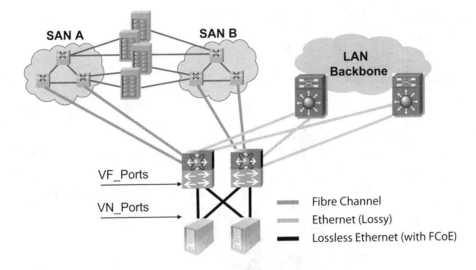

Figure 3-18   Initial FCoE Deployment

Figure 3-20 adds FCoE directly connected storage arrays. From an FCoE perspective there is no real difference between a host and a storage array. The concepts of initiator and target are SCSI concepts, not FC concepts, therefore they do not appear in FCoE.

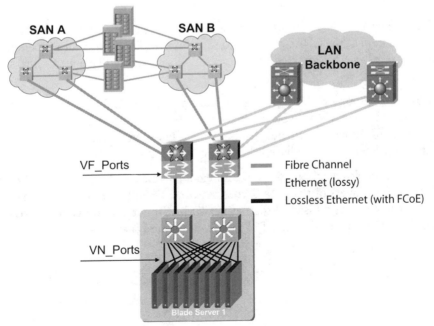

Figure 3-19   Adding Blade Servers

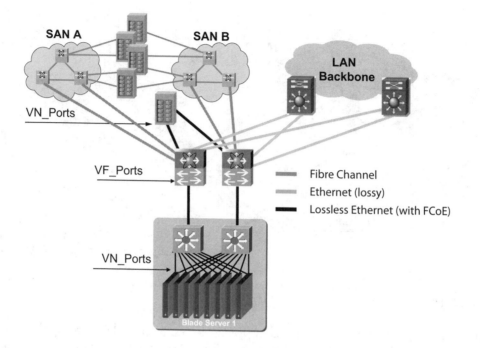

Figure 3-20   Adding Native FCoE Storage

For FCoE, a storage array is just another device that accesses the FCoE network using a CNA. FCoE does not care that the CNA acts as a target or as an initiator. From an FC perspective, an FCoE storage array is a VN_Port that accesses a VF_Port, exactly like a host. This is identical to the native FC model.

Another possible topology is shown in Figure 3-21, where the FC E_Ports between the FCoE switches and the FC switches have been replaced by FCoE VE_Ports. This also shows that it is not only possible for Ethernet switches that implement FCoE to have FC ports, but also for FC switches that implement FCoE to have Ethernet ports.

Many other FCoE deployments are possible, for example to extend the reach of FCoE into the aggregation and core layers of the Data Center network. Yet another example is an end-to-end deployment of FCoE over a losless Ethernet network without native FC connectivity. All of these topologies are supported by the T11 FC-BB-5 standard [13].

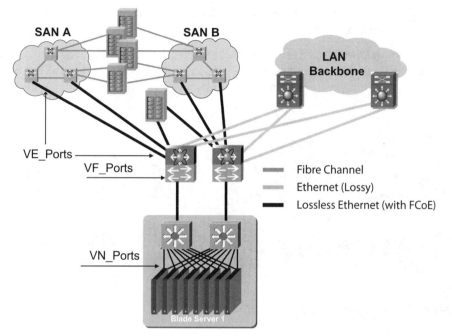

Figure 3-21 Adding VE_Ports

FCoE Addressing

FCoE frames carry two types of addresses: MAC addresses and FC addresses.

They serve two different purposes:

- MAC addresses are used as hop-by-hop addresses from the VN_Port to the VF_Port, or between two VE_Ports, or from a VF_Port to a VN_Port.
- FC addresses (i.e., FC_IDs or N_Port_IDs) are used as end-to-end addresses from the VN_Port of the host to the VN_Port of the storage array or vice versa.

This is consistent with the IP model, where IP addresses are end-to-end and MAC addresses change hop-by-hop.

FC addresses are assigned only to VN_Ports, since they are end-to-end, and this is the reason why they are called N_Port_IDs by the standards. VE_Ports are not explicitly addressed at the FC layer, and therefore they do not have FC addresses.

MAC addresses, being hop-by-hop, are assigned to VN_Ports, VF_Ports, and VE_Ports, since a hop may be the connection between a host and a switch, or between two switches.

Traditional Fibre Channel fabric switches maintain forwarding tables based on FC_IDs. FC switches use these forwarding tables to select the best link available for a frame so that the frame reaches its destination port. Fibre Channel links are typically point-to-point and do not need an address at the link layer.

Ethernet networks are different because Ethernet switches (which are not explicitly addressed) create a "cloud" (i.e., a multi-access network). This requires FCoE to rely on Ethernet MAC addresses to direct a frame to its correct Ethernet destination.

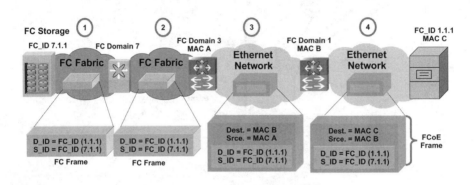

Figure 3-22   Example of FCoE Addressing

Figure 3-22 shows an example of a frame traveling left to right.

On the left is a storage array attached to a Fibre Channel switch labeled FC Domain 7. This storage array is in a traditional SAN and stores information for a host on an FCoE enabled Network. The host has both an FC_ID 1.1.1 and a MAC address C.

The Fibre Channel N_Port on the storage array transmits the FC frame, which includes the Destination FC_ID (D_ID = 1.1.1) and the Source FC_ID (S_ID = 7.1.1) in the FC header (for simplicity, only the header information is displayed in Figure 3-22).

The Fibre Channel switch with Domain ID = 7 receives the frame. Since the destination ID (D_ID) in not in its FC Domain (it is in Domain 1, not in Domain 7), the switch looks up the destination Domain ID in its forwarding table and transmits the frame on the port associated with the shortest path, as determined by the Fabric Shortest Path First (FSPF) protocol.

The switch with the FC Domain ID = 3 receives the frame and determines that the destination ID (D_ID) is not in Domain 3 and performs the lookup process. However, in this case the FC frame is transmitted across an FCoE enabled Ethernet Network. This requires the FC frame to be encapsulated into an Ethernet frame by a switch VE_Port FCoE_LEP and then transmitted on the port associated with the shortest path.

While the original FC source and destination N_Port_IDs are maintained in the encapsulated FC frame, the FCoE_LEP inserts Ethernet and FCoE headers. In the Ethernet header, it populates the destination and source MAC addresses. In the example, the destination MAC address is B (the MAC address of the FCoE_LEP in the receiving switch), and the source MAC address is A (the MAC address of the FCoE_LEP in the transmitting switch).

When the FCoE frame arrives at the FCoE_LEP with MAC address B, the frame is decapsulated and the switch determines that the FC frame destination is within its Domain (Domain ID 1). The FC frame is re-encapsulated with the new destination MAC address C (which corresponds to the FC D_ID 1.1.1), and the source MAC address is set to B. Then the frame is transmitted out of the appropriate port to the FCoE host with destination MAC address C.

When the frame is received by the CNA with MAC address C, the FCoE frame is decapsulated, and the FC frame accepted by the host with FC_ID 1.1.1.

This example demonstrates how traditional FC addresses map to FCoE MAC addresses. Topologies vary depending on a customer's implementation requirements and the FCoE-capable products deployed, but the addressing schemes remain the same.

FCoE Forwarding

To understand how forwarding works in presence of the STP and FSPF, let us consider Figure 3-23.

STP runs on all the Ethernet clouds and prunes them to trees. In this example, we have two spanning trees (STP#1 and STP#2). FSPF runs over the pruned trees and provides end-to-end forwarding at the FC layer. In the example of Figure 3-22 there are no meshes, therefore the two STPs do not prune any link, and FSPF has a single forwarding path.

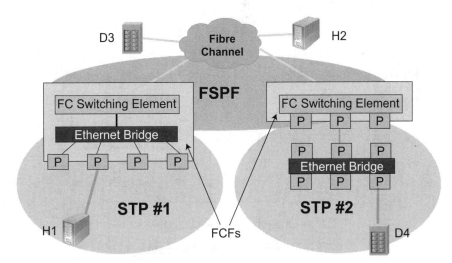

Figure 3-23 STP/FSPF Interaction (1)

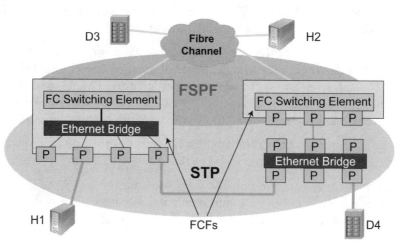

Figure 3-24 STP/FSPF Interaction (2)

Figure 3-24 shows the same topology with an additional link that has caused the two STPs to merge into a single one. The STP does not prune any links, since there are no meshes at the Ethernet layer, but FSPF now sees two alternative paths, a native FC one and an FCoE one: If the metrics are equal, FSPF can balance the traffic between them.

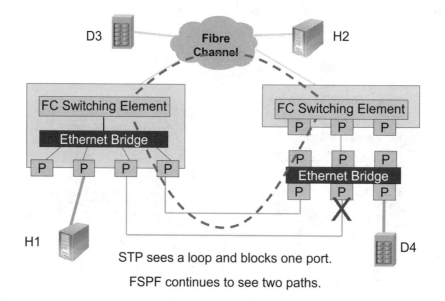

Figure 3-25 STP/FSPF Interaction (3)

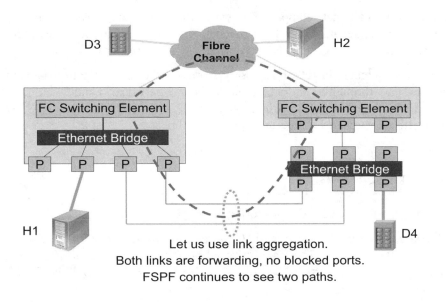

Let us use link aggregation.
Both links are forwarding, no blocked ports.
FSPF continues to see two paths.

Figure 3-26 STP/FSPF Interaction (4)

If an additional Ethernet link is added at the bottom (see Figure 3-25), Ethernet now has a mesh.

STP prunes a link by blocking a port (marked with an "X"). Traffic does not flow over the blocked port, unless the parallel Ethernet link fails. FSPF continues to see two alternative paths only. (i.e., it does not see the blocked link.)

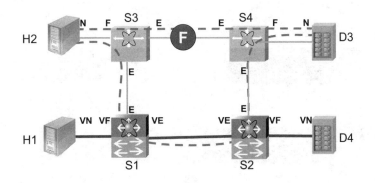

Figure 3-27 Rerouting in the Presence of a Fault

Figure 3-26 shows an alternative approach in which the two parallel links have been grouped using Ethernet link aggregation (i.e., Etherchannel). The two links are both forwarding, since they are seen by STP as a single link. FSPF continues to see two alternative paths only.

Figure 3-27 shows a mixed FC/FCoE topology. Normally the shortest path from H2 to D3 is the straight FC path through S3 and S4, but since the link between S3 and S4 has failed, FSPF reroutes the traffic from H2 to D3 through the path H2 – S3 – S1 – S2 – S4 – D3, which is a mixed path with some native FC links and some FCoE links.

FPMAs and SPMAs

Let us now discuss how MAC addresses for FCoE usage are assigned.

The MAC addresses on an FCF (i.e., the MAC addresses associated to VE_Ports and VF_Ports) are derived from the FCF pool. These are Universal MAC addresses that the FCF manufacturer has bought from IEEE and burned in a Read Only Memory (ROM) inside the FCF. They are worldwide unique.

VN_Ports may use two types of MAC addresses: Fabric Provided MAC Addresses (FPMAs), also called Mapped MAC Addresses, or Server Provided MAC Addresses (SPMAs).

FPMAs follow the FC model in which the FCF (i.e., the fabric) assigns the FC_IDs. FPMAs are MAC addresses assigned by the FCF during the FIP login process (i.e., FIP FLOGI and FIP NPIV FDISC, see page 103). They are not unique worldwide, but the FC fabric guarantees that they are unique within the fabric, as it does for FC_IDs.

SPMAs are based on the idea that MAC addresses belong to the hosts and therefore each host decides which MAC address to use. The uniqueness is delegated to some host management software because with the introduction of virtualization MAC addresses are no longer unique (for example, see [19]).

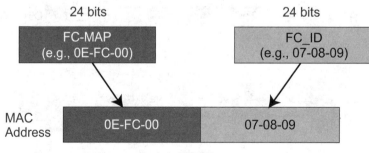

Figure 3-28 Mapped MAC Addresses, or FPMAs

The MAC address scheme and the MAC address value used by each VN_Port are negotiated by FIP (see page 103).

The FC-BB-5 standard [13] allows both FPMAs and SPMAs for VN_Ports. FPMAs are mandatory to implement while SPMAs are optional, to allow all FCoE implementations to interoperate. Initial deployments use only FPMAs while SPMAs are not used.

FPMAs are constructed by concatenating a prefix called FC-MAP (Fibre Channel - MAC Address Prefix) with the VN_Port's FC_ID, as shown in Figure 3-28.

With FPMAs, each FC_ID has its own MAC address that is algorithmically derived and therefore there is no need to store it. Since the FC_ID is assigned by the fabric during the FLOGI or NPIV FDISC process and the FC-MAP is assigned by the fabric in the FIP protocol, the MAC address is assigned by the fabric. This is consistent with the FC model.

The FC-MAP is pragmatically an Organization Unique Identifier (OUI) with U/L bit set to 1 to indicate that it is a Local address, not worldwide unique. The default value is 0EFC00h, and the recommended range is from 0EFC00h to 0EFCFFh.

Since many customers deploy physically separated SAN fabrics, it is possible to assign different values of FC-MAP to each fabric, thus having an additional assurance that there are no addressing conflicts, if two fabrics are accidentally merged together.

An additional advantage of FPMAs is that the MAC address pair also encodes the type of communication (from which port type to which port type), and this adds robustness in the case of erroneous configurations (see Table 3-1). Note that the FC-BB-5 standard supports the first three types of comunications listed in Table 3-1; direct VN_Port to VN_Port Virtual Links are not supported.

Table 3-1   FPMAs Usage with FCoE

Type of Communication	MAC Addresses
VE_Port to VE_Port	DA = Not Mapped
	SA = Not Mapped
VF_Port to VN_Port	DA = Mapped
	SA = Not Mapped
VN_Port to VF_Port	DA = Not Mapped
	SA = Mapped
VN_Port to VN_Port	DA = Mapped
	SA = Mapped

The usage of MAC addresses by VN_Ports is shown in Figure 3-12. Each ENode has a universal MAC address, called ENode MAC address, that is used by the FIP protocol. When FPMAs are used the ENode MAC address is not used for FCoE traffic, each FCoE_LEP has an FPMA mapped from the N_Port_ID of its paired VN_Port. With SPMAs the ENode MAC address may be used also for FCoE traffic, as a MAC address associated with FCoE_LEPs.

FIP: FCoE Initialization Protocol

Correlating Figure 3-12 with Figure 3-8 allows you to understand not only how FCoE preserves the Fibre Channel interactions at the FC-2V sublevel and above, but also how Fibre Channel and FCoE are different at the lower levels.

In Figure 3-8 a point-to-point Fibre Channel link connect the two communicating Fibre Channel ports. A point-to-point link may connect only two points, therefore no special processing is needed to reach the other point: just transmit a frame, and it will reach the other side of the link.

In Figure 3-12 the two Ethernet ports of the two communicating lossless Ethernet MACs are connected through a lossless Ethernet network. This is where FCoE drastically differs from native Fibre Channel: FCoE devices are connected through multi-access networks, not through point-to-point links.

Fibre Channel protocols rely on the point-to-point properties of the physical layer. As an example, when an N_Port is initialized, it just transmits a FLOGI frame; the Switch port at the other end of the point-to-point link receives the frame and replies accordingly. Once the FLOGI is completed, the indication from the physical layer that the link is active is used to maintain VN_Ports and VF_Ports: as long as the physical layer asserts that the link is up the upper level entities are kept; when the physical layer asserts that the link is down the upper level entities are de-instantiated.

In a FCoE environment this is no longer possible; an ENode needs to know the MAC address of the FCF to which to perform the FLOGI in order to be able to encapsulate the FLOGI frame in an Ethernet frame and transmit it over the lossless Ethernet network. Once the FLOGI is completed, different mechanisms are needed to maintain VN_Ports and VF_Ports, because the physical layer provides an indication about the state of the locally attached link, but this information is not sufficient to ensure that a remote entity is still reachable through the lossless Ethernet network.

These challenges are solved by FIP, the FCoE Initialization Protocol, whose main purpose is defining a way to present a multi-access Ethernet network as a set of point-to-point Virtual Links for FCoE use. In particular, FIP solves the following problems:

- **VLAN Discovery:** How ENodes and FCFs discover the FCoE VLANs
- **FCoE Entitites Discovery:** How ENodes and FCFs discover each other over the FCoE VLANs in a lossless Ethernet network

- **Entities instantiation:** How VN_Ports, VF_Ports, and VE_Ports are instantiated, and which MAC addresses are associated to each of them
- **Entities maintenance and de-instantiation:** How to detect a loss of connectivity over a FCoE Virtual Link and how to perform the related de-instantiation of entities

To perform these functions FIP defines the four following protocols:

- FIP VLAN Discovery
- FIP Discovery
- FIP Virtual Link Instantiation
- FIP Virtual Link Maintenance

FIP Messages

Figure 3-29 shows an example of a FIP frame. FIP frames have an Ethertype different than the one used for FCoE frames. The FIP Ethertype is 8914h.

The FIP Protocol Code identifies the FIP protocol to which an FIP message belongs. The FIP Subcode identifies the role of the message in the protocol (e.g., if it is a request or a response).

Destination MAC Address
Source MAC Address
(IEEE 802.1Q Tag)
EtherType = FIP	Ver	Reserved
FIP Protocol Code	Reserved	FIP SubCode
Descriptor List Length	FP SP	Flags	A S F
Descriptor List
(FIP Pad / Ethernet Minimum Length Pad)
Ethernet FCS

Figure 3-29 FIP Frame Format

FIP has been designed to be flexible and extensible. Each FIP frame carries a list of Tag, Length, Value (TLV) structured descriptors in the Descriptor List field, whose length is specified by the Descriptor List Length field.

The FIP Protocol Code, FIP Subcode, and Descriptor List content identify a FIP operation. Each FIP frame carries a FIP operation. Table 3-2 shows the FIP operations.

Table 3-2 FIP Operations

FIP Protocol	FIP Subcode	FIP Operation
0001h	01h	Discovery Solicitation
	02h	Discovery Advertisement
0002h	01h	Virtual Link Instantiation Request
	02h	Virtual Link Instantiation Reply
0003h	01h	Keep Alive
	02h	Clear Virtual Links
0004h	01h	VLAN Request
	02h	VLAN Notification

Each descriptor is encoded with the TLV (Type, Length, Value) syntax. Table 3-3 shows the FIP descriptors.

Table 3-3 FIP Descriptors

Criticality	Type	Descriptor
Critical	1	Priority
	2	MAC Address
	3	FC-MAP
	4	Name_Identifier
	5	Fabric
	6	Max FCoE Size
	7	FLOGI
	8	NPIV FDISC
	9	Fabric LOGO
	10	ELP
	11	Vx_Port Identification
	12	FKA_ADV_Period
	13	Vendor_ID
	14	VLAN
Non-Critical	240 .. 254	Vendor Specific

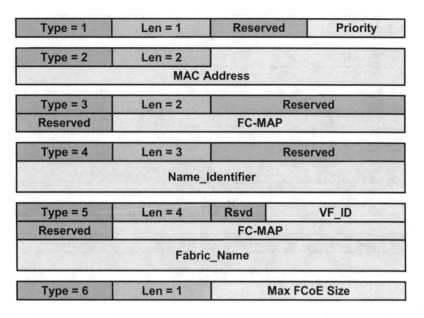

Figure 3-30 FIP Descriptors (1)

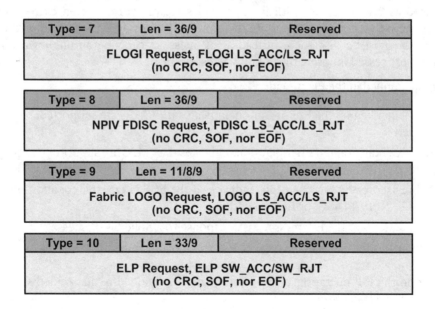

Figure 3-31 FIP Descriptors (2)

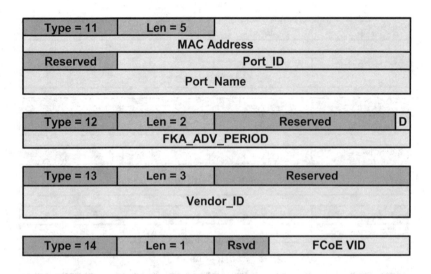

Figure 3-32   FIP Descriptors (3)

FIP descriptors are shown in Figure 3-30, Figure 3-31, and Figure 3-32. Several descriptors are combined together to build the different messages of the FIP protocol. FIP descriptors are classified as critical or noncritical. Critical descriptors are expected to be understood and processed by every implementation; therefore a FIP message carrying an unknown critical descriptor must be discarded. Instead a FIP message carrying an unknown noncritical descriptor is processed ignoring the unknown descriptor.

Five flags are defined in the Flags field:

- **FP:** Depending on the FIP operation, indicates if FPMAs are supported, requested, or granted
- **SP:** Depending on the FIP operation, indicates if SPMAs are supported, requested, or granted
- **A:** In Discovery Advertisements, indicates if the FCF is available for additional FLOGI, NPIV FDISC, or ELP operations
- **S:** Indicates that the FIP message is a response to a Solicitation message
- **F:** Indicates that the FIP message is originated by an FCF

Depending on the FIP operation, a FIP message may be padded to a specified size or to the Ethernet minimum frame size.

FIP VLAN Discovery

Ethernet networks deploy VLANs to separate various subnets or traffic types. The most common deployment model for FCoE is based on having all FCoE traffic in its own VLANs, with one VLAN per FC fabric. This requires an appropriate VLAN configuration on ENodes, which may be cumbersome in certain environments.

The FIP VLAN Discovery protocol allows an administrator to perform the FCoE VLANs configuration on the FCFs of the network. ENodes may use the FIP VLAN Discovery protocol to discover these FCoE VLANs. FCFs may use the FIP VLAN Discovery protocol to verify the VLAN configuration of neighbor FCFs.

The FIP VLAN Discovery protocol is based on two messages, VLAN Request and VLAN Notification. On becoming operational, an ENode may send a VLAN Request to the multicast address All-FCF-MACs using its port VLAN or a VLAN it has available. If an FCF is reachable over that VLAN, it replies with a VLAN Notification message over that VLAN, message carrying the list of FCoE VLAN IDs (VIDs). The ENode uses the returned information to select and configure the VLANs where to access FCoE services. If the administrator changes the FCoE VLANs configuration on an FCF, the FCF may send an unrequested VLAN Notification message to the ENodes logged in with it, to provide them the updated FCoE VLANs configuration.

Figure 3-33 shows the descriptor list carried in an FIP VLAN Request message. The Name_Identifier descriptor is optional. If included it allows the FCF to reply after applying additional policies related to the requester.

Figure 3-34 shows the descriptor list carried in an FIP VLAN Notification message.

FIP Protocol Code = 0004h		Reserved	SubCode = 01h	
Descriptor List Length = 5 or 2			Flags	F
Type = 2	Len = 2			
Requester's MAC Address				
Type = 4	Len = 3		Reserved	
Requester's Name_Identifier				

Figure 3-33   FIP VLAN Request

FIP Protocol Code = 0004h		Reserved	SubCode = 02h
Descriptor List Length = n+2		Flags	F
Type = 2	Len = 2		
FCF-MAC Address			
Type = 14	Len = 1	Rsvd	FCoE VID #1
Type = 14	Len = 1	Rsvd	FCoE VID #2
Type = 14	Len = 1	Rsvd	FCoE VID #n

Figure 3-34   FIP VLAN Notification

FIP Discovery

The FIP Discovery protocol allows ENodes to discover FCFs to establish VN_Port to VF_Port Virtual Links, and FCFs to discover other FCFs to establish VE_Port to VE_Port Virtual Links. The protocol is based on Advertisement messages, sent by FCFs, and on Solicitation messages, sent by ENodes and FCFs.

VF_Port capable FCF-MACs periodically send Advertisements to the Ethernet multicast address All-ENode-MACs. On receiving these Advertisements, ENode FCoE Controllers create an entry per FCF-MAC in a FCF List. ENode FCoE Controllers select a subset of the available FCF-MACs for Login (the FCF Login Set) based on a local policy.

Each FCF-MAC belonging to the FCF Login Set needs to be verified for jumbo frame support on the Ethernet path before performing the FLOGI. This is accomplished by sending a unicast Solicitation to the FCF-MAC and receiving a jumbo unicast Advertisement in response. After this step, the ENode is able to perform the FIP FLOGI with that FCF-MAC.

When an ENode FCoE Controller becomes operational, it can just wait to receive the Advertisements and operate as described above. However this may take some time, therefore an ENode FCoE Controller, when it becomes operational, should send a multicast Solicitation to the Ethernet multicast address All-FCF-MACs. FCF-MACs respond with jumbo unicast Advertisements. On receiving these Advertisements, the ENode FCoE Controller may proceed directly to the FIP FLOGI phase.

The same process works for VE_Port capable FCF-MACs, with the difference that they send periodic Advertisements to the Ethernet multicast address All-FCF-MACs.

Figure 3-35 shows the descriptor list of a Solicitation message sent by an ENode. This Solicitation includes a MAC address descriptor, carrying the ENode MAC address, a Name_Identifier descriptor, carrying the ENode Node_Name, and a Max FCoE Size descriptor, carrying the maximum size the ENode intends to use for FCoE PDUs. This maximum size is used in solicited unicast Advertisements to verify the support for this size for FCoE frames (e.g., baby jumbo frames) by the Lossless Ethernet network.

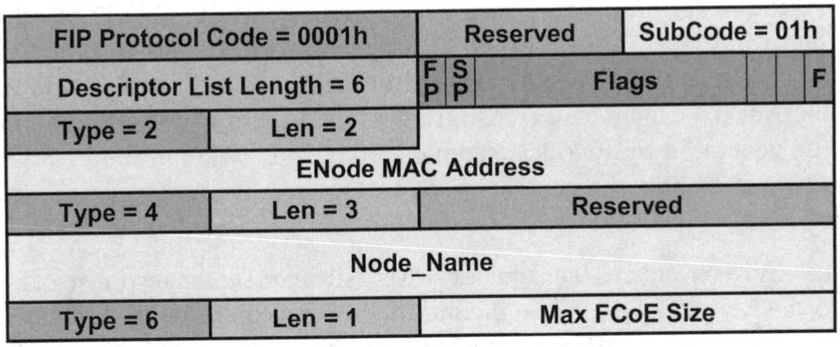

FIP Protocol Code = 0001h		Reserved	SubCode = 01h
Descriptor List Length = 6	F S P P	Flags	F
Type = 2	Len = 2		
ENode MAC Address			
Type = 4	Len = 3	Reserved	
Node_Name			
Type = 6	Len = 1	Max FCoE Size	

Figure 3-35 FIP Solicitation from an ENode

In this solicitation message the F flag is equal to zero, since the message is not generated by an FCF. The FP and SP flags indicate the MAC address scheme supported by the ENode (at least one of the two bits must be set).

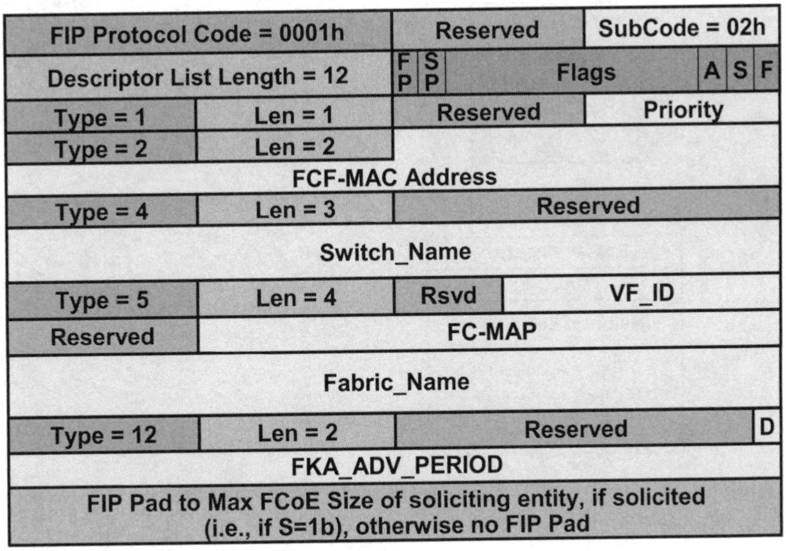

FIP Protocol Code = 0001h		Reserved	SubCode = 02h
Descriptor List Length = 12	F S P P	Flags	A S F
Type = 1	Len = 1	Reserved	Priority
Type = 2	Len = 2		
FCF-MAC Address			
Type = 4	Len = 3	Reserved	
Switch_Name			
Type = 5	Len = 4	Rsvd	VF_ID
Reserved		FC-MAP	
Fabric_Name			
Type = 12	Len = 2	Reserved	D
FKA_ADV_PERIOD			
FIP Pad to Max FCoE Size of soliciting entity, if solicited (i.e., if S=1b), otherwise no FIP Pad			

Figure 3-36 FIP Advertisement

Figure 3-36 shows the descriptor list of an Advertisement message. An Advertisement includes a Priority descriptor, carrying an administratively configurable priority for the originating FCF-MAC, a MAC address descriptor, carrying the FCF-MAC address, a Name_Identifier descriptor, carrying the FCF Switch_Name, a Fabric descriptor, and an FKA_ADV_Period descriptor. The Fabric descriptor carries the VF_ID of the Fabric (i.e., the VSAN ID), if any, the Fabric's FC-MAP value, used to construct FPMAs addresses, and the Fabric_Name. The FKA_ADV_Period descriptor carries the period according to which periodic Advertisements are transmitted by FCFs and FIP Keep Alive messages are expected to be generated by ENodes (see page 108). The D flag in the FKA_ADV_Period descriptor allows to disable the generation of FIP Keep Alive messages over directly connected links.

Solicited unicast Advertisements (i.e., unicast Advertisements sent in response of a Solicitation) are padded to the Max FCoE Size specified in the Solicitation to which they are responding. Reception of solicited unicast Advertisements by an ENode is then an indication that the Lossless Ethernet network supports the appropriate jumbo frame size for FCoE. Solicited unicast Advertisements have the S flag set to one.

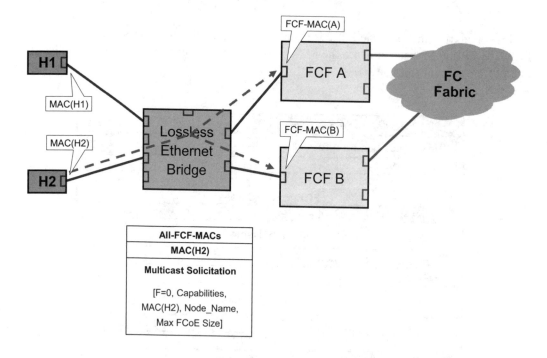

Figure 3-37 Multicast Solicitation from H2

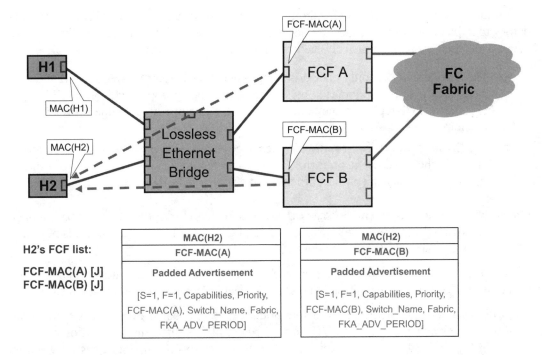

Figure 3-38 Unicast Advertisements from A and B

Unsolicited Advertisements (i.e., Advertisements sent periodically by FCF-MACs) are always multicast and do not carry any FIP Pad. Unsolicited multicast Advertisements have the S flag set to zero.

The F flag is set to one in FIP Advertisements. The A flag is set to one to indicate that the originating FCF-MAC is able to accept additional FIP FLOGI or FIP NPIV FDISC requests. The FP and SP flags indicate the MAC address scheme supported by the FCF (at least one of the two bits must be set).

Figure 3-37 shows an example of the Discovery Solicitation phase. H2 sends a multicast Solicitation message carrying the descriptor list shown in Figure 3-35 to the multicast MAC address All-FCF-MACs. This message reaches both FCFs (FCF-A and FCF-B). They individually reply with a solicited unicast Advertisement.

Figure 3-38 shows the unicast Advertisements sent by FCF-A and FCF-B in reply to the Solicitation from H2. Since they are unicast, they reach only H2 but not H1. In other words, an FCF generates specific solicited unicast Advertisements for each soliciting ENode. The FCF may also not reply to an ENode solicitation (e.g., because the capabilities of the ENode and of the FCF do not match, or because of security policies).

Let us now discuss how the FP and SP bits are set. For interoperability reasons FPMAs are mandatory to implement; however, they are not mandatory to use. (For example, an administrator may disable their use.) The protocol is generic and handles two cases:

- The ENode supports only one addressing scheme (i.e., either SPMA or FPMA). It indicates this in the Solicitation by setting to one the appropriate bit (either FP or SP) and the FCF replies to the Solicitation only if it supports the same addressing scheme.

- The ENode supports both addressing schemes. It sets both bits to one in the Solicitation. In the Advertisement, if the FCF has a preference, it sets to one only one bit, deciding which scheme to use, otherwise it sets to one both bits.

On receiving the Advertisement messages, the ENode builds a list of the FCFs that have replied with the associated capabilities and priorities (H2's FCF List in Figure 3-38). At this point the ENode can establish VN_Port to VF_Port Virtual Links.

The ENode selects one or more FCFs from the list, according to its capabilities and configuration policies. For High Availability (HA) it should select at least two FCFs and log into them.

The FIP Discovery protocol is used also among VE_Port capable FCF-MACs to discover each other to establish VE_Port to VE_Port Virtual Links. A different Solicitation message, shown in Figure 3-39, is used in this case. The F bit set to one distinguishes between an ENode generated Solicitation and an FCF generated Solicitation. An FCF generated Solicitation carries also an FC-MAP descriptor in addition to the descriptors carried in an ENode generated Solicitation because the FC-MAP value has to be consistent across a Fabric. A receiving FCF ignores this Solicitation if the received FC-MAP does not match the FCF's FC-MAP.

FIP Protocol Code = 0001h		Reserved	SubCode = 01h	
Descriptor List Length = 8	F P / S P	Flags		F
Type = 2	Len = 2			
FCF-MAC Address				
Type = 3	Len = 2	Reserved		
Reserved	FC-MAP			
Type = 4	Len = 3	Reserved		
Switch_Name				
Type = 6	Len = 1	Max FCoE Size		

Figure 3-39 FIP Solicitation from an FCF

FIP Virtual Link Instantiation

In native Fibre Channel, VN_Ports, VF_Ports, and VE_Ports are instantiated on successful completion of FLOGI, NPIV FDISC, and ELP Exchanges.

In FCoE, a VN_Port to VF_Port Virtual Link is instantiated on successful completion of a FIP FLOGI Exchange or of a FIP NPIV FDISC Exchange. The FLOGI or NPIV FDISC ELSs are carried inside a FIP frame to augment their original functionality with the capability of negotiating the VN_Port MAC addresses.

Using FIP makes it easy for intermediate Ethernet bridges intercepting these messages. Ethernet bridges must monitor FIP to open and close Access Control Lists (ACLs) to protect the storage traffic from intentional or unintentional (erroneous configuration) attacks.

The FIP Virtual Link instantiation messages are identified by the FIP Protocol Code, the FIP SubCode, and by the particular descriptor carried (i.e., type 7 for FLOGI, type 8 for NPIV FDISC, type 9 for Fabric LOGO, type 10 for ELP).

Figure 3-40 shows the descriptor list of a FIP FLOGI Request message. A FIP FLOGI Request message carries an FLOGI descriptor and a MAC address descriptor. The setting of the FP and SP bits and the MAC address contained in the MAC address descriptor depends on the addressing mode the ENode is requesting the FCF to use:

- If the ENode is requesting the FCF to use FPMAs (i.e., FP=1, SP=0), the MAC address in the MAC address descriptor is set to zero.

- If the ENode is requesting the FCF to use SPMAs (i.e., FP=0, SP=1), the MAC address in the MAC address descriptor is set to the MAC address the ENode is proposing to use as VN_Port MAC address.

- If the ENode is leaving the decision of which addressing scheme to use to the FCF (i.e., FP=1, SP=1), the MAC address in the MAC address descriptor should be set to the MAC address the ENode is proposing to use as VN_Port MAC address in case the FCF chooses to operate with SPMAs.

FIP Protocol Code = 0002h		Reserved	SubCode = 01h
Descriptor List Length = 38	FP SP	Flags	
Type = 7	Len = 36	Reserved	
FLOGI Request (no CRC, SOF, nor EOF)			
Type = 2	Len = 2		
Proposed MAC Address			

Figure 3-40 FIP FLOGI Request

FIP Protocol Code = 0002h		Reserved	SubCode = 02h
Descriptor List Length = 38	F S P P	Flags	
Type = 7	Len = 36	Reserved	
FLOGI LS_ACC (no CRC, SOF, nor EOF)			
Type = 2	Len = 2		
Granted MAC Address			

Figure 3-41   FIP FLOGI LS_ACC

Figure 3-41 shows the descriptor list of a FIP FLOGI LS_ACC message. A FIP FLOGI LS_ACC message carries an FLOGI descriptor and a MAC address descriptor. The MAC address descriptor carries the MAC address the FCF assigned to the just logged in VN_Port. The FP and SP bits specify which addressing scheme has to be used. (i.e., only one of the two bits is set.)

Figure 3-42 shows how ENode H2 can send multiple FIP FLOGI Requests to multiple FCFs from a single Ethernet port, due to the multi-access nature of the Lossless Ethernet network.

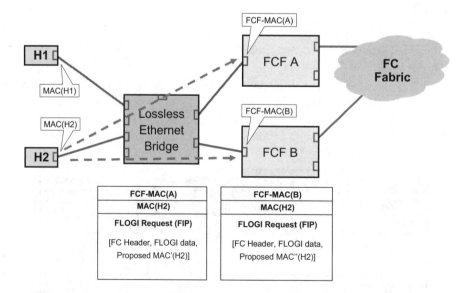

Figure 3-42   FIP FLOGI Request in Action

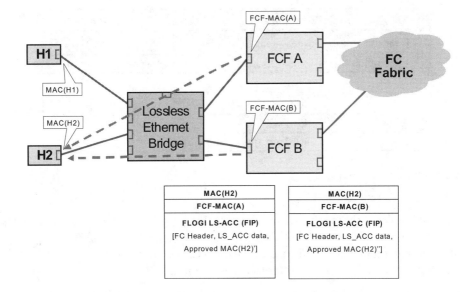

Figure 3-43   FIP FLOGI LS_ACC in Action

Figure 3-43 shows the flow of FIP FLOGI LS_ACC messages generated by FCFs upon accepting the FIP FLOGI Request.

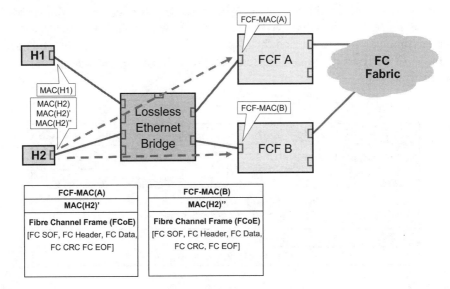

Figure 3-44   Established VN_Port to VF_Port Virtual Links

FIP Protocol Code = 0002h			Reserved		SubCode = 01h
Descriptor List Length = 35			Flags		
Type = 10	Len = 33		Reserved		
ELP Request (no CRC, SOF, nor EOF)					
Type = 2	Len = 2				
MAC Address (to be used)					

Figure 3-45 FIP ELP Request

In practice, the Lossless Ethernet bridges redirect the FIP protocol to their management engines to transparently set up the proper FCoE ACLs, while they switch the FCoE frames in hardware as regular Ethernet frames. The purpose of FCoE ACLs is to make the Virtual Links more robust over the Ethernet network. It is not to enforce zoning policies.

Receiving the FIP FLOGI LS_ACC messages concludes the instantiation of the VN_Port to VF_Port Virtual Link and the ENode can start sending regular FC frames using FCoE as shown in Figure 3-44. Note that the notation MAC(H2)' and MAC(H2)" indicates that H2 uses two different FPMAs, one to communicate with FCF A and one to communicate with FCF B.

To instantiate a VE_Port to VE_Port Virtual Link a FIP ELP Exchange is used, involving a FIP ELP Request and a FIP ELP SW_ACC messages. The process is very similar to the one to instantiate a VN_Port to VF_Port Virtual Link, however the MAC addresses are just communicated and not negotiated, and the FP and SP flags are not used. Figure 3-45 shows the descriptor list of a FIP ELP Request message. Figure 3-46 shows the descriptor list of a FIP ELP SW_ACC message.

FIP Protocol Code = 0002h			Reserved		SubCode = 02h
Descriptor List Length = 35			Flags		
Type = 10	Len = 33		Reserved		
ELP SW_ACC (no CRC, SOF, nor EOF)					
Type = 2	Len = 2				
MAC Address (to be used)					

Figure 3-46 FIP ELP SW_ACC

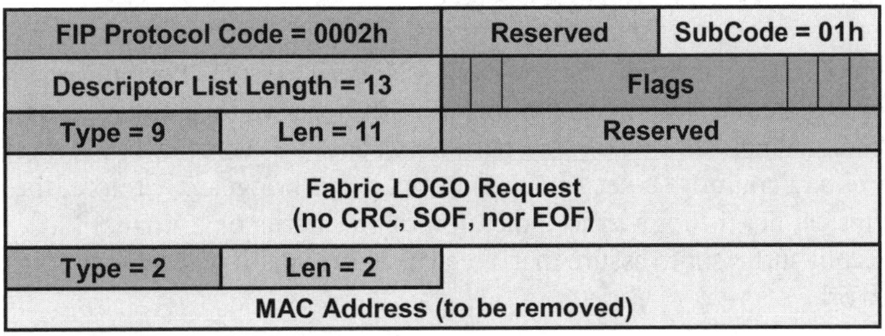

FIP Protocol Code = 0002h		Reserved	SubCode = 01h
Descriptor List Length = 13		Flags	
Type = 9	Len = 11	Reserved	
Fabric LOGO Request (no CRC, SOF, nor EOF)			
Type = 2	Len = 2		
MAC Address (to be removed)			

Figure 3-47   FIP Fabric LOGO Request

VN_Ports are usually associated with an OS/Hypervisor or with virtual machines. If a virtual machine is shut down, the associated VN_Port has to be de-instantiated as well. Fibre Channel uses the Fabric LOGO process for that (i.e., sending a LOGO ELS to the Fabric Controller Well Known Address). This process is leveraged for FCoE, by encapsulating the Fabric LOGO ELS in FIP. This allows the removal of the MAC address associated with the VN_Port being de-instantiated.

Figure 3-47 shows the descriptor list of a FIP Fabric LOGO Request. Figure 3-48 shows the descriptor list of a FIP Fabric LOGO LS_ACC.

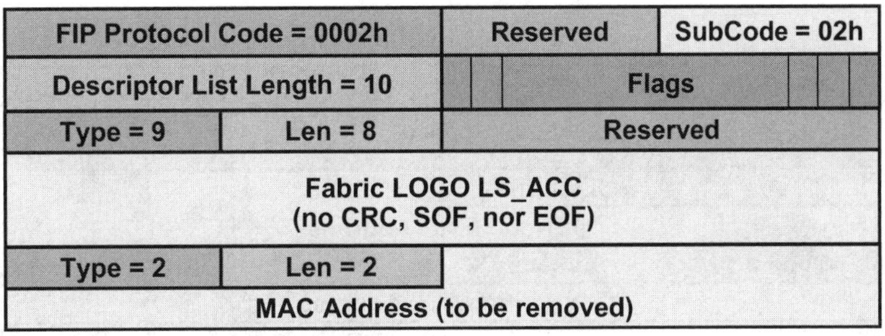

FIP Protocol Code = 0002h		Reserved	SubCode = 02h
Descriptor List Length = 10		Flags	
Type = 9	Len = 8	Reserved	
Fabric LOGO LS_ACC (no CRC, SOF, nor EOF)			
Type = 2	Len = 2		
MAC Address (to be removed)			

Figure 3-48   FIP Fabric LOGO LS_ACC

FIP Virtual Link Maintenance

In native Fibre Channel, the link connecting a VN_Port to a VF_Port and the link connecting two VE_Ports are physical links, and therefore they derive their state (up or down) by the physical layer signaling. With FCoE, the path between a VF_Port and a VN_Port or between two VE_Ports may comprise a set of Ethernet links and bridges. Therefore, the status of an individual physical link is not a valid indication of the status of a Virtual Link, because this information is not sufficient to assure that a remote entity is still reachable through the lossless Ethernet network.

In FCoE, the state associated to a VN_Port, VF_Port, or VE_Port has to be verified through a control protocol and cannot be inferred by the physical layer signaling. FC-BB-5 has chosen a "soft state" approach (i.e., an approach where if periodic Keep Alive messages are not received, then a Virtual Link is de-instantiated).

The FCoE Controller performs the following maintenance function:

■ It monitors the "health" of VN_Ports, VF_Ports, and VE_Ports and generates appropriate periodic Keep Alive messages on behalf of them.

■ It maintains timers per each appropriate entity to de-instantiate it, if some consecutive Keep Alive messages are not received.

On ENodes, the reception of periodic multicast Advertisements allows FCoE Controllers to continuously verify that a VF_Port is reachable. After two missing Advertisements the VF_Port is considered unreachable and the associated VN_Ports are de-instantiated.

FIP Protocol Code = 0003h		Reserved		SubCode = 01h
Descriptor List Length = 7 or 2			Flags	
Type = 2	Len = 2			
ENode MAC Address				
Type = 11	Len = 5			
VN_Port MAC Address				
Reserved		N_Port_ID		
N_Port_Name				

Figure 3-49   FIP Keep Alive Message

An ENode FCoE Controller generates periodic unicast FIP Keep Alive messages on behalf of itself with a periodocity equal to FKA_ADV_PERIOD. This value is provided by FCFs in FIP Advertisements to allow the FCF-MAC to verify the connectivity with that ENode and be able to react in case of loss of connectivity. An ENode FCoE Controller also generates periodic unicast FIP Keep Alive messages at a lower fixed frequency per each VN_Port to allow the remote FCF-MAC to verify the health of the VN_Ports and to keep the forwarding tables of intermediate Ethernet bridges updated.

On FCFs, the reception of periodic unicast FIP Keep Alive messages allows FCoE Controllers to continuously verify that an ENode or a VN_Port is reachable. After two missing FIP Keep Alive messages the ENode or VN_Port is considered unreachable and the associated FCoE_LEP(s) are de-instantiated.

Figure 3-49 shows the descriptor list of a FIP Keep Alive message. There are two variants of FIP Keep Alive messages: ENode FIP Keep Alive messages and VN_Port FIP Keep Alive messages.

ENode FIP Keep Alive messages carry only a MAC address descriptor and are sent with the ENode MAC address as source address.

VN_Port FIP Keep Alive messages carry a MAC address descriptor and a Vx_Port Identification descriptor, identifying the VN_Port they are sent on behalf of. VN_Port FIP Keep Alive messages are sent with the VN_Port MAC address as source MAC address.

FIP Keep Alive messages are not used to verify the state of VE_Port to VE_Port Virtual Links. The periodic unsolicited multicast Advertisements provide the information needed.

FIP Protocol Code = 0003h		Reserved		SubCode = 02h
Descriptor List Length = (n*5)+5			Flags	
Type = 2	Len = 2			
FCF-MAC Address				
Type = 4	Len = 3		Reserved	
Switch_Name				
Type = 11	Len = 5			
VN_Port MAC Address #1				
Reserved		N_Port_ID #1		
N_Port_Name #1				
...				
Type = 11	Len = 5			
VN_Port MAC Address #n				
Reserved		N_Port_ID #n		
N_Port_Name #n				

Figure 3-50 FIP Clear Virtual Links Message to an ENode

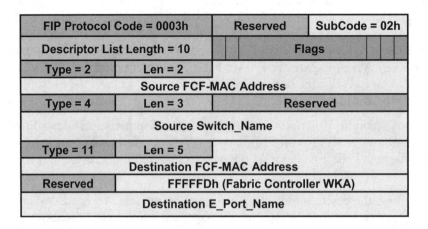

Figure 3-51 FIP Clear Virtual Links Message to an FCF

The Virtual Link Maintenance protocol defines another FIP message to allow an FCF to explicitly de-instantiate remote VN_Ports or VE_Ports, the FIP Clear Virtual Link message. In a sense, it is the counterpart of the Fabric LOGO function a VN_Port can invoke, but on the FCF side. As an example, a VF_Port capable FCF-MAC may detect that a VF_Port is not operational and needs to tell the logged in ENode to de-instantiate all the VN_Ports logged in with that VF_Port. A FIP Clear Virtual Link message identifies several VN_Ports to be de-instantiated.

Figure 3-50 shows the descriptor list of a FIP Clear Virtual Link message sent by an FCF to an ENode. Such a message carries a MAC address descriptor and a Name_Identifier descriptor, to identify the originating FCF-MAC, and a list of Vx_Port Identification descriptors, each identifying a specific VN_Port to be de-instantiated.

Figure 3-51 shows the descriptor list of a FIP Clear Virtual Link message sent by an FCF to another FCF. Such a message carries a MAC address descriptor and a Name_Identifier descriptor, to identify the originating FCF-MAC, and one Vx_Port Identification descriptor, identifying the remote VE_Port to be de-instantiated.

Converged Network Adapters

Converged Network Adapter (CNA) is the commercial name for an ENode. A CNA is usually a PCI Express adapter that contains both the functions of traditional HBAs and NICs. CNAs are available as regular PCI Express boards and in mezzanine form factor for the server blades of blade server systems.

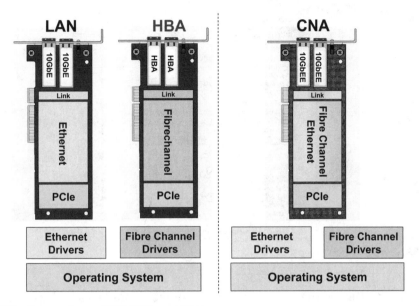

Figure 3-52 Comparison of NIC, HBA, and CNA

CNAs will soon start to appear on motherboards, an arrangement often called LAN On Motherboard (LOM). This will make FC even more mainstream in the Data Center, since it will be basically available "for free" on the motherboard.

The initial CNA vendors are the today's HBA vendors. The most common structure of a CNA is illustrated in Figure 3-52.

The interesting aspect of this architecture is that the view from the operating system is of two separate devices that run standard drivers: a dual port Ethernet adapter and a dual port Fibre Channel HBA.

From a SCSI perspective, the host is not capable of distinguishing that SCSI is running over FCoE instead of over FC.

From an FC perspective, the only additional component is the FIP protocol that is implemented by the FCoE controller inside the CNA or in the CNA drivers.

Management tools can run unmodified, since they still see FC; over time, they will be extended to be able also to monitor the Ethernet component of FCoE.

Figure 3-53 shows an example of how Microsoft Windows sees a CNA:

■   In the "Network Adapters" section of the Control Panel it sees two Ethernet NICs.

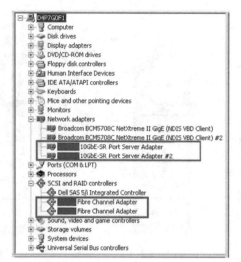

Figure 3-53   How Windows Sees a CNA

- In the "SCSI and RAID controllers" section of the Control Panel it sees two Fibre Channel Adapters.

Since the CNAs are manufactured by the same companies that manufacture HBAs, they are the first host solution to be certified by the storage array vendors.

However, in the medium term the NIC vendors will also offer FCoE capabilities and start to sell CNAs. This will reshape the overall NIC/HBA/CNA market.

FCoE Open Software

FCoE can also be implemented entirely in software. This may be particularly interesting for servers that perform non-I/O intensive operations but that have the need to access the storage arrays.

A complete software implementation of FCoE exists in the public domain in an open-source project available at http://www.Open-FCoE.org/ [16]. Software implementations have started to appear in Linux distributions like RedHat or SuSE and in Microsoft Windows.

The software architecture of this project is shown in Figure 3-54. On the left side there is the simplified software architecture of a storage stack over a CNA; on the right side is the open FCoE software architecture.

Applications not only are unaware of running over FCoE instead of FC, but they are also unaware that FCoE is implemented in software.

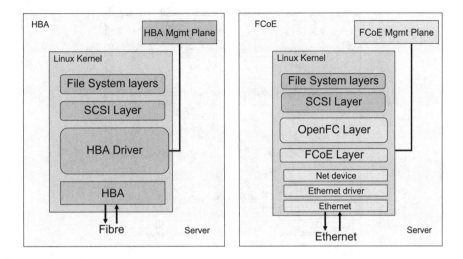

Figure 3-54   Open-FCoE Software

This approach clearly loads the CPU more than in the case of a CNA but is predicated on the fact that with advent of multicore CPUs, "CPU cycles are abundant" and some can be spared for FCoE.

This approach does not require any particular hardware, just the classical NIC available on the motherboard.

Network Tools

A variety of network tools, both commercial and public domain, is available to analyze, debug, and troubleshoot FCoE. Among the public domain tools, it is worth mentioning Wireshark.

Wireshark (http://wireshark.org/) is the most used public domain protocol analyzer, previously known as Ethereal. It captures and displays network traffic, and it has been extended to provide a full decode of FCoE.

Figure 3-55 shows a screenshot of Wireshark while decoding an ELS PRLI FC frame carried over FCoE.

Example traces can be downloaded from

- http://wiki.wireshark.org/SampleCaptures

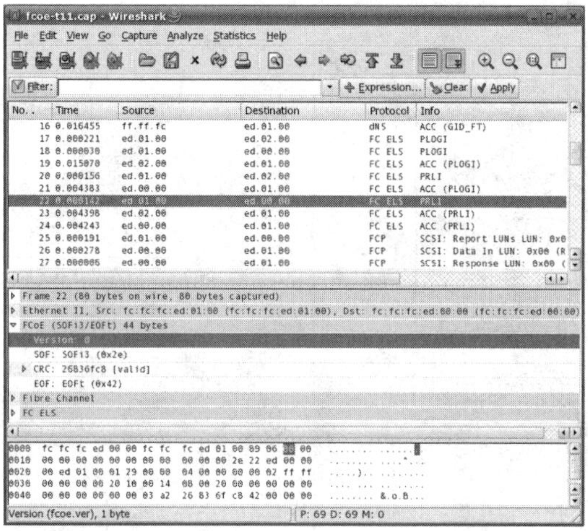

Figure 3-55   Wireshark Screen Shot

FCoE and Virtualization

The capability of effectively utilize multiple cores per processors (i.e., multicore CPUs) and multiple processors per servers (i.e., multisocket servers) is often delegated to virtualization software.

Virtualization makes it possible to run multiple operating systems and multiple applications on the same computer at the same time, increasing hardware utilization.

Virtualization software is available on the market for different processors and applications. The most commonly known software are VMware, Linux XEN, and Hyper-V from Microsoft. They differ in their architectures and features; however, they all have the concept of a Virtual Machine (VM), an instance of an operating system and applications, which shares the HW resources (CPU, Memory, I/O) with other VMs. This allows running several operating systems and applications, at the same time, on a single server in a safe and controlled manner.

The virtualization software typically achieves this by inserting a thin layer of software directly on the computer hardware or on a host operating system. This software layer (normally called hypervisor) creates VMs, allocates hardware resources to VMs, monitors the health of the VMs, and participates in their movement from one system to another. Figure 3-56 shows the classical arrangement of VMs and hypervisor.

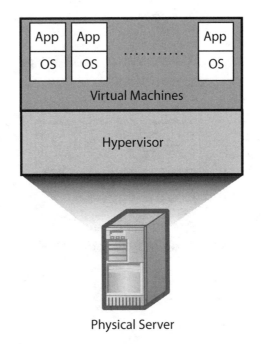

Figure 3-56   VMs and Hypervisor

Effective virtualization deployments depend on storage being decoupled from servers. This is normally achieved with either a Fibre Channel or an iSCSI SAN. This ensures that each VM has immediate access to any file system, enabling immediate movements of the VMs by eliminating the time-consuming copying of OS, applications, and files from one server to another.

In this new virtualized world, to decide how to insert FCoE, it is interesting to understand how block I/O works, and where FC and iSCSI are currently terminated.

Fibre Channel Block I/O

Fibre Channel I/O is typically terminated in the hypervisor, where the drivers of the HBAs run, as shown in Figure 3-57, dashed circle A.

Historically the hypervisor owned one port WWN (pWWN) per physical HBA port and used it to perform a single FLOGI to an FC switch. Using the FLOGI performed by the hypervisors, the VMs are capable of reaching multiple targets (i.e., storage arrays) and multiple LUNs (volumes) inside each target.

This mode posed a limitation on the zoning capability, since the only entity known to the FC network was the hypervisor (i.e., physical server), not the VMs. In other words, since all the VMs shared the same FLOGI, they were indistinguishable from the FC network point of view.

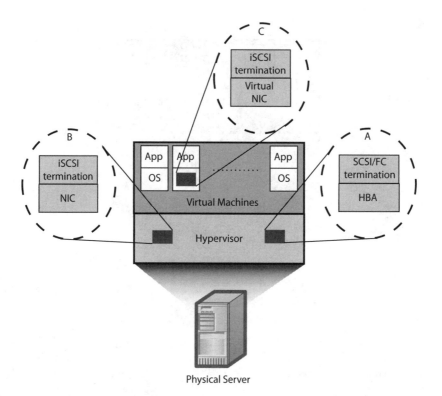

Figure 3-57   Examples of Block I/O Termination

Recent developments added to the hypervisors the capability to perform N_Port_ID Virtu-alization (NPIV). With NPIV a single Fibre Channel HBA port can login into the FC fabric multiple times by using different pWWNs. This allows the creation of multiple VN_Ports, one per VM, each with its own Fibre Channel address (FC_ID). In this mode, each VM appears as a unique entity on the Fibre Channel fabric and can be zoned independently.

iSCSI Block I/O

iSCSI is a block I/O protocol based on TCP/IP. It can be implemented either in hardware, by iSCSI-capable NICs, or in software.

Hardware implementations are similar to the Fibre Channel ones: The NIC drivers run in the hypervisor where iSCSI is terminated. The hypervisor can use a single iSCSI session for the entire physical server or one per VM (see Figure 3-57, dashed circle B).

Since iSCSI can also be terminated in software, another possibility exists: iSCSI can be run in the VM, over a Virtual NIC, see Figure 3-57, dashed circle C. The hypervisor is completely unaware of this, since the iSCSI traffic is just TCP traffic as the traffic used by all the other applications.

Moving a VM

VM movements are coordinated between hypervisors. When a movement operation is ready to start, the hypervisor quiesces the block I/O, provides time for the pending I/O operations to complete and then moves the VM. This results in no frames lost for storage traffic and therefore in no timeouts at the SCSI layer.

This applies to both FC and iSCSI, when terminated in the hypervisor, independently of the number of open sessions.

When iSCSI is terminated in the VM, things work slightly different, since the VM has no notion of movements' boundaries. If the VM is moved while iSCSI transactions are pending, immediately after the move IP frames associated to iSCSI are incorrectly delivered to the old location. iSCSI deals with this situation correctly, since the TCP layer detects that the frames are missing and ask for retransmission. The SCSI layer does not see any frame drop, and the session is not aborted and does not timeout.

FCoE and Block I/O

FCoE can deal with block I/O exactly like FC does (i.e., by terminating FCoE/FC in the hypervisor; see Figure 3-58, dashed circle A). This solution is expected to be supported by VMware and CNA vendors by the time this book is published. This solution can be achieved either by using a CNA or by running the FCoE software stack in the hypervisor. As in the native FC case, a single FLOGI can be used for the whole server, or NPIV can be deployed to identify the different VMs. In the case of VM movement, the hypervisors take care of quiescing the I/O and doing the movements, and no frames are lost, as in the FC case.

FCoE can also be terminated in a VM, using the software stack over a Virtual NIC (see Figure 3-58 dashed circle B). The behavior here is different from iSCSI, since FCoE does not use TCP but lossless Ethernet.

This requires a lossless Ethernet vNIC in the VM and a lossless virtual Ethernet bridge in the hypervisor. In addition, lossless Ethernet is "lossless" in normal operation, but in the presence of a topology change, frames can be lost. The movement of a VM implies the movement of the MAC and IP addresses associated with the VM. This is a form of topology change. While these addresses move and before they are advertised in the new location, in-flight frames continue to be delivered to the old location. This may cause a few frames to be lost and the protocol that will recover them is SCSI itself, for example after aborting the in-flight SCSI sequences, without waiting for a timeout period.

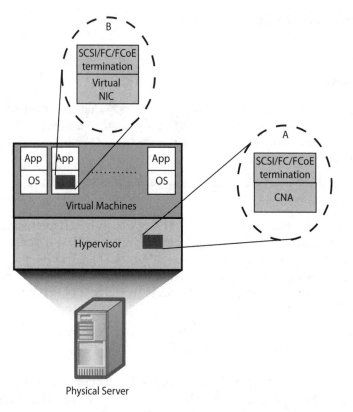

Figure 3-58   FCoE termination and Virtualization

FCoE FAQ

In spending time evangelizing FCoE to industry and to customers, we noticed that there are few questions that periodically pop up. We will try to answer them in the following sections.

Is FCoE Routable?

Allow us to reply with a question: Are you sure this is the question you want to ask, or is it instead "Is FCoE IP routable?"

The answer to the second question is clearly: NO!

It is evident, by looking at Figure 3-59, that FCoE does not have an IP layer, and therefore it is not IP routable. This was not an oversight; it was a conscious design decision. As the famous French writer Antoine de Saint-Exupery (1900 to 1944) used to say: "Perfection is achieved, not when there is nothing more to add, but when there is nothing left to take away."

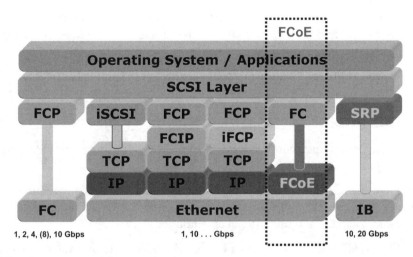

Figure 3-59   Comparison of Storage Stacks

FCoE is simple, and it provides what is needed to carry FC over Ethernet and nothing else.

The industry has already developed other standards to carry FC over IP, in particular FCIP (see Figure 3-59). FCIP is "IP routable" and it is already part of the same FC-BB-5 standard that defines also FCoE.

Figure 3-60 shows a disaster tolerant solution in which two Data Centers that use FCoE are connected with an IP network using FCIP.

Data that need to be sent to a remote site traverse an FCIP link via a gateway and similarly enter an FCoE network via an FCIP gateway. File backups to tape libraries and recovery from these devices continue to use existing backup and recovery tools.

Coming back to the original question "Is FCoE routable?" Another possible answer is "FCoE, like FC, can be routed by FCoE switches." FCoE switches may forward FC frames across different Ethernet clouds according to the destination FC_ID.

Figure 3-60   FCoE and FCIP

Soon we will start to see on the market multiprotocol routers that implement the FCF functionality in addition to IPv4 and IPv6 routing (similar to the one depicted in Figure 3-61).

Figure 3-61 shows that the IPv4 and IPv6 routers operate across VLANs, while each FCF operates inside a VLAN. Multiple FCFs are interconnected by an IFR (Inter-Fabric Routing) module.

iSCSI Versus FCoE?

iSCSI and FCoE are two important technologies that Cisco supports to provide Unified Fabric solutions.

The value proposition of Unified Fabric is well understood: It dramatically reduces the number of adapters on the servers, the number of switch ports, and the associated cabling; it improves airflow, and reduces capital, and operational expenditures.

Servers with dual 10GE connectivity into a Unified Fabric have a good value proposition. The Data Center Bridging (DCB) collection of Ethernet improvements makes Ethernet even more appealing. These improvements can be beneficial at both Layer 2 and Layer 3 transports and are therefore valuable independently of the I/O consolidation technique used: iSCSI, FCoE, NAS, or, more likely, some combination of them.

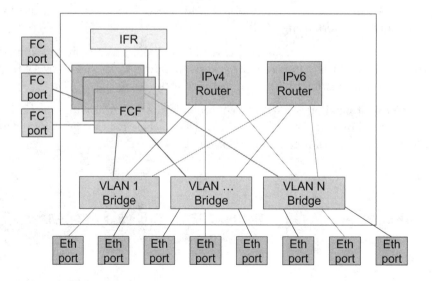

Figure 3-61   Multiprotocol Router with FCoE Capability

Internet SCSI (iSCSI) is a mature technology created by the Internet Engineering Task Force (IETF) in the IP Storage (IPS) working group. It is based on the IP protocol stacks, it assumes (as IP does) an underlying unreliable network, and it delegates to TCP the recovery of lost packets.

Fibre Channel over Ethernet (FCoE) is a new technology originally developed by Cisco and now defined in the FC-BB-5 standard of INCITS T11. Most large Data Centers have a huge installed base of Fibre Channel and want a technology that maintains the FC model. FCoE assumes a "lossless Ethernet" in which frames are never dropped (as in Fibre Channel) and therefore does not use IP and TCP.

A comparison of the protocol stacks is illustrated in the Figure 3-59.

iSCSI fits well with the SMB market where often price is more of a concern than performance. iSCSI can use legacy Ethernet switches; FCoE requires lossless switches. Up to now iSCSI has been limited to the low performance servers, mainly because Ethernet had a maximum speed of 1 Gbit/s, while FC HBAs had 2 Gbps and 4 Gbps interfaces.

This is even more relevant for iSCSI storage arrays, where a 1 GE interface is typically shared by multiple servers to be cost effective. iSCSI gateways with 4GFC interfaces have been deployed to overcome the bottleneck represented by the backend array connection.

10GE has removed this limitation, but there are concerns that the TCP termination required by iSCSI is onerous at this speed.

For some Enterprise customers, with a large installed base of FC, the downside is that iSCSI is SCSI over TCP, it is not FC over TCP, and therefore it does not preserve the management and deployment model of FC. It has a different naming scheme (perhaps a better one, but anyhow different), different zoning, and so on.

In contrast, FCoE integrates seamlessly into an existing FC environment. FCoE is simple and it contains the minimum indispensable to carry FC over Ethernet and nothing else.

One of the biggest changes that is happening in the Data Center is the adoption of virtualization (e.g., VMware and XEN). Virtualization is a way to consolidate multiple underutilized logical servers on few physical servers. Virtualization dramatically increases the I/O requirement and this seems to create another opportunity for FC and FCoE since they do not require the TCP stack and therefore are not subject to TCP/IP overhead.

With virtualization comes virtual machine mobility that often requires Layer 2 connectivity. This fits well with the DCB extensions, since DCB provides better Layer 2 Ethernet, and it is therefore synergistic with FCoE.

In practice, whether FCoE is faster than iSCSI is going to be as much a function of the particular implementation of the technology as anything inherent to the protocols themselves.

In term of storage arrays, native iSCSI storage arrays have existed for some time. Native FCoE storage arrays have been shown by different companies and will become commercial products in the short term.

In summary:

■ FCoE was not designed to kill iSCSI. There are many applications where iSCSI is better suited and FCoE is not applicable. This is particularly true in lower end systems and in small remote branch offices, where IP connectivity is of paramount importance.

■ Some customers have limited I/O requirements in the 100 Mbps range, and iSCSI is just the right solution for them: This is why iSCSI has taken off and is so successful in the SMB market, because it is cheap and it gets the job done.

■ Large Enterprises are embracing virtualization, have much higher I/O requirements, and want to preserve the investments and training in Fibre Channel: For them FCoE is probably a better solution.

■ Customers that have adopted Cisco MDS switches will probably prefer FCoE as it guarantees natural coexistence with Fibre Channel with no need to migrate existing FC infrastructures.

■ FCoE will take a large share of the SAN market. FCoE will not kill iSCSI, but it will likely reduce its potential market.

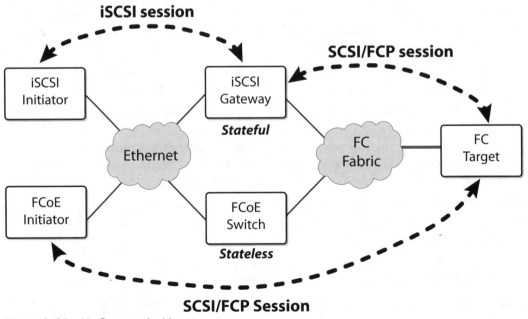

Figure 3-62   No Gateway Architecture

Does FCoE Require Gateways?

The answer is no: FCoE is not a new storage architecture; it is just a new physical layer for Fibre Channel.

SCSI continues to be mapped over FC, as in classical Fibre Channel, and there is an encapsulation layer (called FCoE) to encapsulate FC over Ethernet.

The encapsulation/decapsulation functions, performed by the FCoE_LEPs inside the FCoE switches and CNAs, simply add or remove an Ethernet envelope around an FC frame. The FC frame is untouched, and the operation is completely stateless. This is the reason for requiring 2.5 KB jumbo frames: FCoE does not implement fragmentation nor reassembly.

The FCoE_LEP has its own MAC address, but the FC_ID and the WWNs continue to reside in the overlaying VN_Ports, as shown in Figure 3-10.

Figure 3-62 attempts to clarify why FCoE does not require gateways by comparing it to iSCSI. A similar comparison applies to SRP over Infiniband.

In iSCSI there is not an end-to-end FCP session. It is split in an iSCSI session between the initiator and the gateway (that acts as a target and has an identity) and in an FCP session between the iSCSI gateway and the FC target. The iSCSI gateway presents itself as an initiator over the FC fabric, mapping the iSCSI initiators to FC initiators. If this mapping is dynamic, the iSCSI initiator is associated to a temporary WWN, and zoning cannot be enforced in FC. If the mapping is static, zoning can be enforced in FC, but the storage administrator must maintain a static mapping table.

Protocol translation, segmentation and reassembly, and error recovery happen at the iSCSI gateway. The iSCSI gateway needs to keep state for each FCP session, requiring memory, and CPU resources.

In FCoE the FCP session is end-to-end, and therefore the FCoE initiator presents itself on the FC fabric with its pWWN. This allows zoning to be used unchanged, independently of the fact that the initiators or the targets are connected to FCoE or FC. The FCoE switch does not keep state for each FCP session. In addition, the FCoE switch does not implement segmentation and reassembly or protocol conversion.

FCoE networks and FC networks can be fully meshed in any arbitrary topology and FSPF always determines the best path between the initiator and the target. This is not true in iSCSI when iSCSI gateways are present.

As a final remark, iSCSI can be deployed end-to-end without gateways, but this implementation does not integrate with Fibre Channel.

Chapter 4

Case Studies

Introduction

This section illustrates possible adoption scenarios of I/O consolidation solutions based on Ethernet and FCoE (see page 67).

Figure 4-1 depicts the common architecture of current Data Centers.

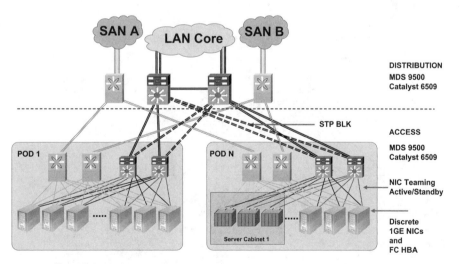

Figure 4-1   Current Data Center Environment

The servers at the bottom of the picture have multiple 1 Gigabit Ethernet (1GE) cards that are typically configured in NIC teaming (also known as bonding). These cards connect to access layer Ethernet switches like the Catalyst 6509 that can be configured at Layer 2 (bridging only) or at Layer 3 (IP routing). These Ethernet switches are typically aggregated at a higher level by distribution switches that are normally configured to operate at Layer 3 (i.e., IP routers). The distribution Ethernet switches may also host service blades for firewalling, load balancing, and intrusion detection. They connect to the LAN core (i.e., to the Intranet) and through it possibly to the Internet.

The same servers are equipped with HBAs and connected to Fibre Channel access switches like the MDS 9500. The Fibre Channel topology normally consists of two separates fabrics (SAN-A and SAN-B) not interconnected. The access layers switches are connected to FC distribution layer switches (i.e., FC directors).

I/O consolidation is particularly valuable in the connection of servers to the access switches. In fact, this allows a strong reduction of the number of interface cards to be installed in the servers, and of number and types of cables and switch ports.

I/O Consolidation with Discrete Servers

Figure 4-2 shows a first attempt at I/O consolidation in a Data Center that uses discrete rack mounted servers. CNAs are installed on the servers, and the Ethernet and FC access layer switches have been consolidated into FCoE switches (in the example, the Cisco Nexus 5000).

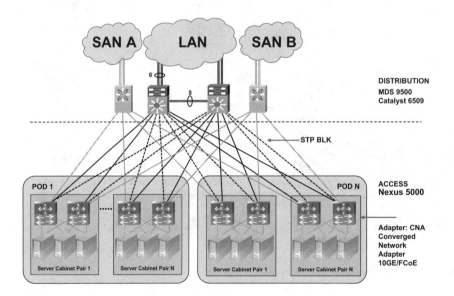

Figure 4-2 I/O Consolidation with Spanning Tree

The I/O from the server to the FCoE switches is consolidated over 10GE (for example, using copper Twinax cables).

The FCoE switches operate at Layer 2, since this greatly simplifies the movement of Virtual Machines in the Data Center. (That is, the MAC and IP addresses can be easily moved inside Layer 2 domains.)

The distribution layer is unchanged. The FC uplinks from the FCoE switches plug into the FC SAN-A and SAN-B, which are two separate SANs. Two separate instances of FSPF run: one on SAN-A and the other on SAN-B. Each instance manages its topology, and all the FC links are active and forward traffic.

Depending on the customer preference, the Nexus 5000 in the access layer may operate either as FCFs (FCoE Forwarders) or as FIP snooping bridges (i.e., Ethernet bridges transparently monitoring FIP traffic in order to generate automatically FCoE ACLs).

When acting as FCFs, the Nexus 5000 switches act as FC switches (i.e., they acquire domain IDs, participate in the principal switch selection, run FSPF, enforce zoning, act as name servers, and distribute RSCN information). In this case, the FC ports between the access layer and the distribution layer are either E_Port (if the links are FC) or VE_Ports (if the links are Ethernet).

When acting as FIP snooping bridges, the Nexus 5000 switches act as a funnel toward an FC switch; they do not acquire domain IDs; they just pass all the control protocols to the upstream FC switches. If the link between the access switches and the distribution switches are FC links, this mode of operation on the access switch is called NPV (N_Port Virtualizer) proxy; the port on the distribution switch is an F_Port, and the port on the access switch is an N_Port. If the link between the access switches and the distribution switches are Ethernet links, this mode of operation on the access switch is called FIP snooping, the ports on the distribution switches are VF_Ports, and the one on access switches are VN_Ports.

The situation is different on the Ethernet side, where there is a single LAN backbone.

By default, the Spanning Tree Protocol (STP) runs on the Ethernet meshes present between the access and the distribution layer switches. STP prunes the Ethernet meshes to a tree, by blocking Ethernet ports. Links connected to blocked ports do not carry any traffic. This can be mitigated by running STP per VLAN and by blocking different links on different VLANs, thus load balancing the traffic.

Blocked ports can be avoided in four different ways:

- Enabling Ethernet Host Virtualizer (EHV) on the access switches
- Enabling Virtual Switch (VSS) on the distribution switches
- Enabling virtual Port Channel (vPC) on the distribution switches
- By running Layer 2 Multi-Path (L2MP) between the access switches and the distribution switches

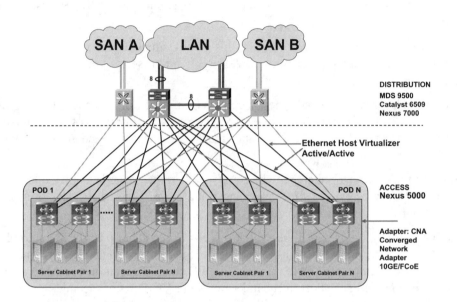

Figure 4-3   I/O Consolidation with Ethernet Host Virtualizer

Figure 4-3 shows an I/O consolidation scenario with Ethernet Host Virtualizers (see page 36). When configured in this mode, the access switches do not forward the traffic received from the distribution switches back to the distribution switches: They do not create meshes. The hosts connected to the access switches are statically load-balanced among the Ethernet uplinks. This operation is often called pinning. The resulting effect is that there is no need to run STP between the access layer and the distribution layer. STP still runs to protect from erroneous configurations, but it does not see any mesh, and therefore it does not prune any links. All the links remain in a forwarding state.

Implementations pay particular attention to how the multicast and broadcast traffic is forwarded to avoid creating broadcast storms and duplicating broadcast/multicast frames.

Figure 4-4 shows an alternative way to skin the cat. In this configuration the distribution switches are configured in Virtual Switch (VSS) or virtual Port Channel (vPC) mode, and therefore they present themselves to the outside world as a single switch. This allows the access switches to use Etherchannel (i.e., Link Aggregation), since they cannot tell that they are speaking to two separate boxes. This particular configuration of Etherchannel is also called Multi-Chassis Etherchannel (MCEC).

Etherchannel load balances the traffic on all the links that are aggregated by using some hash function that normally considers fields in the Layer 2 and Layer 3 headers.

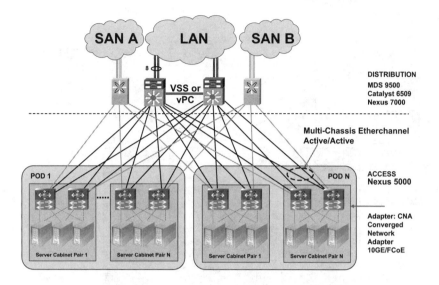

Figure 4-4   I/O Consolidation with VSS and Etherchannel

Again, the STP does not see any mesh, since it considers each Etherchannel a single link and therefore does not prune any link.

Top-of-Rack Consolidated I/O

The three previous solutions lead to an implementation that uses top-of-rack switches. The reason is that the Twinax cable presents a strong economical convenience; it rationalizes nicely and simplifies the server cabling, but it is limited to 10 meters (33 feet).

With this distance limitation, it is possible to connect servers located in one to five racks. The number of servers per rack is a function of the power and cooling infrastructure of the Data Center. Typical numbers go from 10 servers (approx. 5 KW) to 20 servers (approx. 10 KW) per rack.

For example, the Cisco Nexus 5000 has a configuration dedicated to interconnect 40 servers (not all cables are shown). Figure 4-5 shows a configuration with 10 servers per rack that uses four racks. A similar configuration can be obtained in two racks with 20 servers per rack.

Two Nexus 5000 are installed as top-of-rack switches and the servers are equipped with dual ports CNAs. One port is connected to one Nexus 5000 and the other to the other Nexus 5000.

The two Nexus 5000 are then connected to a common LAN for the native Ethernet traffic but to two separate SANs for the FC traffic.

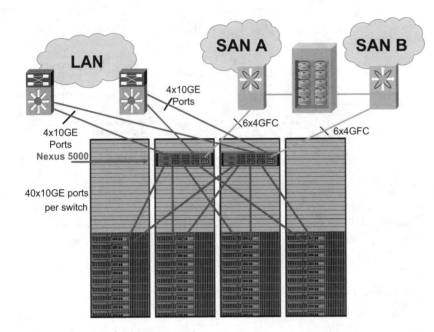

Figure 4-5   Physical Topology: Example with 40 Servers

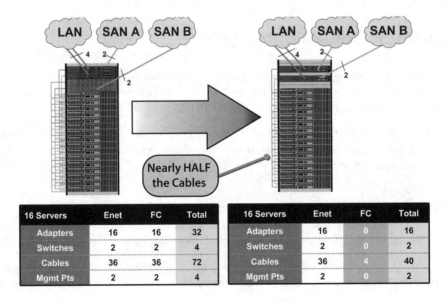

16 Servers	Enet	FC	Total
Adapters	16	16	32
Switches	2	2	4
Cables	36	36	72
Mgmt Pts	2	2	4

16 Servers	Enet	FC	Total
Adapters	16	0	16
Switches	2	0	2
Cables	36	4	40
Mgmt Pts	2	0	2

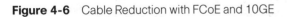

Figure 4-6   Cable Reduction with FCoE and 10GE

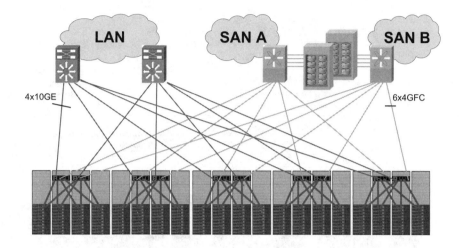

Figure 4-7   Physical Topology: Example with 200 Servers

The Distribution switches can be placed at the end of the row and, even if the distance is greater than 10 meters and the connection therefore requires fiber optics, the cost of the optics is subdivided on a pool of servers, and therefore it is not so critical.

Let us try to estimate the cabling saving of this solution. Figure 4-6 contains an example in which it is possible to see that the number of adapters is clearly divided by 2 and the number of cables is reduced from 72 to 40. The number of cables is not exactly half, since the cables that connect the distribution switches are not consolidated.

Figure 4-7 shows that to build a large pool of servers it is sufficient to repeat the basic building block numerous times.

Using distribution switches with 128 ports total, of which 100 ports are dedicated to connect access switches, it is possible to build a server pool with 1000 servers. With larger port count in the distribution layer switches, or a larger number of distribution switches, it is possible to build even larger server pools.

Example with Blade Servers

What is explained in the previous examples applies to blade servers as well. A blade server is an enclosure that provides power, cooling, and interconnectivity to a set of server blades.

Blade servers may host switch blades capable of switching Ethernet, Fibre Channel, or Infiniband.

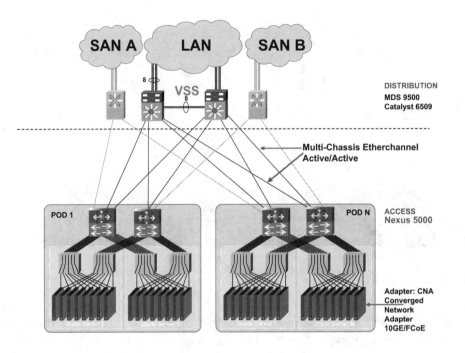

Figure 4-8   Blade Servers: Example with Copper Pass-Through

Figure 4-8 shows an example of blade servers in which no switch blades are installed, but the connectivity is provided through copper pass-through modules. Pass-through modules are passive cards that present one Twinax connection on the outside for each server blade in the blade server.

In this configuration nothing really changes compared to the previous examples: The servers have a different form factor, nothing else.

Figure 4-9 shows blade servers equipped with two 10GE Ethernet switches.

Compared to Figure 4-8 there are the following differences:

■ The number of cables between the blade servers and the access switches is reduced, since the Ethernet switches perform statistical multiplexing of traffic, for example by a factor of two or four.

■ The number of access switches is reduced by the same factor, since fewer ports are needed at the access layer.

■ Local switching among server blades can be enabled, even if sometimes it is problematic to enforce consistent policies when part of the switching happens in the blade servers.

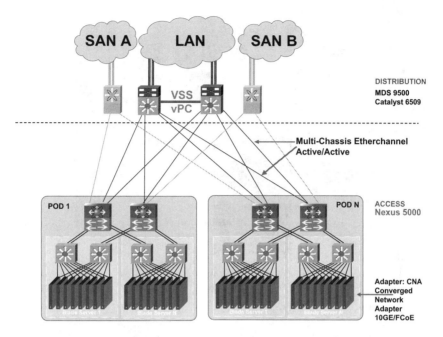

Figure 4-9   Blade Servers: Example with Pure Ethernet Switch

- The cost of the Ethernet switch in the blade server is higher than the cost of the pass-through module.
- The Ethernet switch in the blade server is an additional element that requires management.

Figure 4-10 shows a rack with two Nexus 5000 and two blade servers, each with 10 server blades and two Ethernet switch blades. Each blade server uses one 10GE uplink from each Ethernet switch blade to each Nexus 5000. This is an extreme example of traffic multiplexing but, if more bandwidth is desired, additional links can be inserted in parallel and configured in Etherchannel.

Figure 4-11 shows five racks, each one with two blade servers connected to a pair of Nexus 5000 using Twinax cabling.

Again, this can be repeated multiple times to create larger server pools.

Updating the Distribution Layer

Figure 4-12 shows a possible evolution of the distribution layer limited to the Ethernet portion.

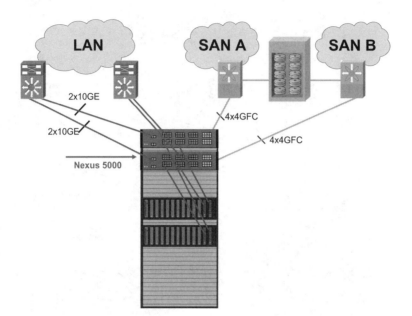

Figure 4-10　Physical Topology: Example with 20 Server Blades

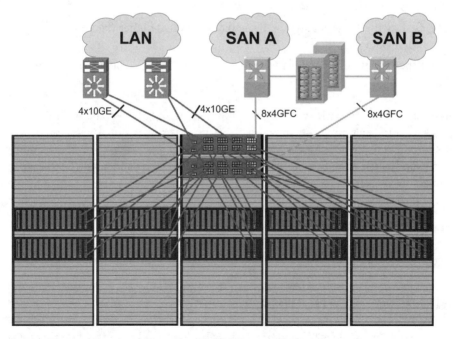

Figure 4-11　Physical Topology: Example with 100 Server Blades

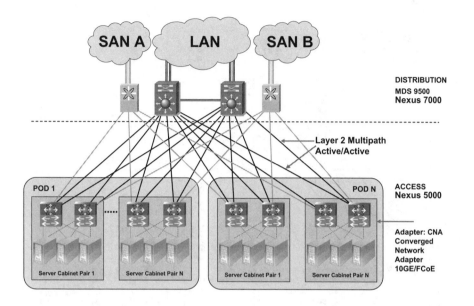

Figure 4-12   Ethernet Layer 2 Multipath

The Catalyst 6509 can be replaced by the larger and more powerful Nexus 7000, which also supports L2MP (Layer 2 Multi-Path). The STP protocol can be eliminated between the access and the distribution layer, greatly increasing and rationalizing the bandwidth available.

L2MP may be extended into the LAN core or a combination of MCEC, and L2MP may be deployed according to needs. This configuration still maintains the SAN traffic from the LAN traffic separate on the backbone.

The last step (shown in Figure 4-13) is to remove this limitation and use a single physical backbone potentially partitioned into multiple logical backbones (SAN-A, SAN-B, LAN) to carry all the traffic.

To achieve this result the Nexus 7000 implements also the FCF functionality, and therefore the connections with SAN-A and SAN-B are moved from the access layer to the distribution layer.

MDS switches are still present for the following reasons:

- To provide connectivity with the legacy native Fibre Channel environment
- To host FCIP gateways required to interconnect multiple data centers
- To host iSCSI gateways to interconnect iSCSI servers
- To provide Inter-VSAN routing (IVR)

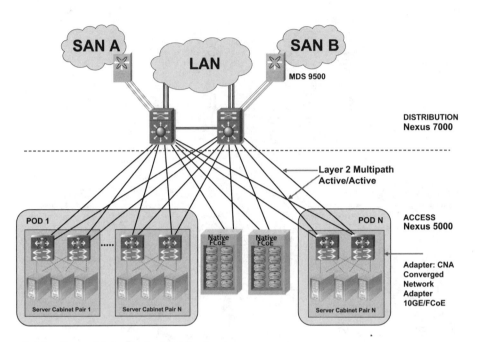

Figure 4-13   Consolidation in the Distribution Layer

■   To provide additional Fibre Channel services like SCSI write acceleration, SAN-TAP, and LUN virtualization

It is clearly desirable to share switches between LAN and SAN, and it is possible to share links. A more conservative installation may decide to share the switches but to use dedicated links for SAN and LAN to achieve a higher degree of traffic separation.

This still saves money, since each port in a switch can be simply configured through management to act either as a pure Ethernet port or as an FCoE port. It eliminates the need to provide separate switches, cables, and optics for the FC networks.

Figure 4-13 illustrates also the interconnection of native FCoE storage arrays to the distribution switches. This solution becomes natural when the I/O is consolidated using FCoE at the distribution layer.

Unified Computing System

The Cisco Unified Computing System (UCS, also known as Project California) is an attempt to eliminate, or at least reduce, the limitations present in current server deployments.

Unified Computing unifies network virtualization, storage virtualization, and server virtualization into one architecture, using open industry standard technologies and with the network as the platform.

UCS is a component of the Cisco Data Center 3.0 architecture. It is a scalable compute platform based on the natural aggregation point that exists in any Data Center: the network.

UCS is composed of "Fabric Interconnects" that aggregate a set of blade chassis.

Compared to blade servers this is an innovative architecture. It removes unnecessary switches, adapters, and management modules. (That is, it has 1/3 less infrastructure compared to classical blade-servers.) This results in less power and cooling and fewer management points that lead to increased reliability.

The Fabric Interconnects can be connected to access layer switches or to distribution switches. The second arrangement is shown in Figure 4-14 and it is more common, since a UCS can contain up to 320 blades.

The Fabric Interconnects (FI1 and FI2 in Figure 4-14) can operate as Ethernet Host Virtualizers (i.e., end-host mode) or as Ethernet switches. In the latter case MCEC is typically used to connect them to the distribution switches.

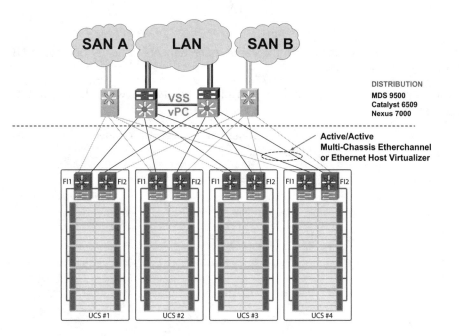

Figure 4-14   UCS Connected to Distribution Switches

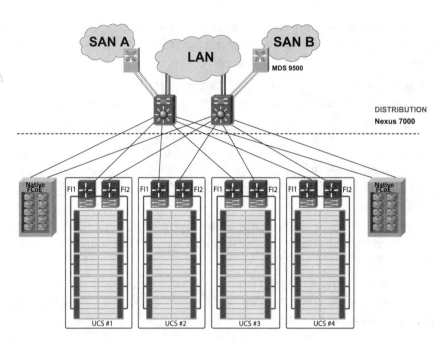

Figure 4-15   UCS with Upstream I/O Consolidation

From the Fibre Channel perspective the Fabric Interconnects typically operate in NPV proxy mode to save FC domain IDs.

As in the previous case, it is possible to consolidate the I/O between the Fabric Interconnect and the distribution switches, as shown in Figure 4-15.

As in the previous case, native FCoE storage arrays can be connected to the distribution switches or directly to the Fabric Interconnects.

Bibliography

PCI Express

[1]   http://computer.howstuffworks.com/pci-express.htm

[2]   http://en.wikipedia.org/wiki/Pci_express

[3]   http://www.pcisig.com/news_room/08_08_07/

IEEE 802.3

[4]   http://standards.ieee.org/getieee802/802.3.html

IEEE 802.1

[5]   http://www.ieee802.org/1/pages/dcbridges.html

[6]   http://www.ieee802.org/1/pages/802.1bb.html

[7]   http://www.ieee802.org/1/pages/802.1az.html

[8]   http://www.ieee802.org/1/pages/802.1au.html

Ethernet Improvements

[9]   SFF-8431–"Enhanced 8.5 and 10 Gigabit Small Form Factor Pluggable Module" ftp://ftp.seagate.com/sff/SFF-8431.PDF

[10]   http://www.cisco.com/en/US/prod/collateral/switches/ps9441/ps9670/white_paper_c11-465436.html

Fibre Channel

[11]   INCITS Project T11/1861-D, Fibre Channel – Framing and Signaling - 3 (FC-FS-3)

[12]   Weber, R., et al., "Fibre Channel (FC) Frame Encapsulation," RFC 3643, December 2003

FCoE

[13]   ANSI INCITS 462:2009, Fibre Channel - Backbone - 5 (FC-BB-5)

[14]   http://www.fcoe.com/

[15]   http://www.t11.org/

[16]   http://www.open-fcoe.org/

[17]   http://www.fibrechannel.org/OVERVIEW/FCIA_SNW_FCoE_WP_Final.pdf

TRILL

[18]   http://www.ietf.org/html.charters/trill-charter.html

Virtualization

[19]   http://www.vmware.com/support/esx21/doc/esx21admin_MACaddress.html

Glossary

- 10GBASE-T: A standard for 10 Gigabit Ethernet over twisted pair cabling.
- 10GE: 10 Gigabit Ethernet, see also IEEE 802.3.
- 802.1: An IEEE standard for LAN Bridging & Management.
- 802.1Q: An IEEE standard for bridges, VLANs, STP, Priorities.
- 802.3: The Ethernet standard.
- ACL: Access Control List, a filtering mechanism implemented by switches and routers.
- aka: also known as.
- AQM: Active Queue Management, a traffic management technique.
- B2B: Buffer-to-Buffer, as in Buffer-to-Buffer credits for FC, a technique to not lose frames.
- BCN: Backward Congestion Notification, a congestion management algorithm.
- Blade Servers: Computer servers with a modular design optimized to minimize the use of physical space.
- CAM: Context Addressable Memory.
- CEE: Converged Enhanced Ethernet, a term used to indicate an evolution of Ethernet.
- CNA: Converged Network Adapter, the name of a unified host adapter that support both LAN and SAN traffic.
- Congestion: The situation when a link or node is carrying so much data that queueing delay, packet loss, or blocking occur.
- CRC: Cyclic Redundancy Check, a function used to verify frame integrity.
- DCB: Data Center Bridging, a set of IEEE standardization activities.
- DCBX: Data Center Bridging eXchange protocol, a configuration protocol.
- DCE: Data Center Ethernet, a term used to indicate an evolution of Ethernet.
- dNS: The Fibre Channel distributed Name Server.
- DWRR: Deficit Weighted Round Robin, a scheduling algorithm to achieve bandwidth management.
- ENode: A host or a storage array in FCoE.
- E_Port: Expansion Port – a port on a Fibre Channel Switch connecting to another Fibre Channel Switch.
- ETS: Enhanced Transmission Selection.
- F_Port: A Fibre Channel port that connects to an N_Port.
- FC: Fibre Channel.

- FC-BB-5: The working group of T11 that standardized FCoE.
- FC_ID: Fibre Channel address, more properly N_Port_ID.
- FC-MAP: Fibre Channel MAC Address Prefix.
- FCC: Fibre Channel Congestion Control, a Cisco technique.
- FCF: FCoE Forwarder, a component of an FCoE switch.
- FCIP: Fibre Channel over IP, a standard to carry FC over an IP network.
- FCoE: Fibre Channel over Ethernet.
- FCS: Frame Check Sequence, a function used to verify frame integrity.
- FIP: FCoE Initialization Protocol.
- FLOGI: Fabric Login.
- FPMA: Fabric Provided MAC Address.
- FSPF: Fibre Channel Shortest Path First.
- HBA: Host Bus Adapter, the adapter that implements the Node functionality in a host or in a storage array.
- HCA: Host Channel Adapter, the IB adapter in the host.
- HDLC: High-Level Data Link Control, a serial protocol.
- HOL blocking: Head Of Line blocking, a negative effect that may cause congestion spreading.
- HPC: High Performance Computing.
- IB: Infiniband, a standard network for HPC.
- IEEE: Institute of Electrical and Electronics Engineers (www.ieee.org).
- IEEE 802.1Qau: An IEEE 802.1 project standardizing Congestion Notification.
- IEEE 802.1Qaz: An IEEE 802.1 project standardizing ETS and DCBX.
- IEEE 802.1Qbb: An IEEE 802.1 project standardizing Priority-based Flow Control (PFC).
- IETF: Internet Engineering Task Force (www.ietf.org).
- IP: Internet Protocol.
- IPC: Inter Process Communication.
- IPv4: Internet Protocol version 4.
- IPv6: Internet Protocol version 6.
- iSCSI: Internet SCSI (i.e., SCSI over TCP/IP).
- ISO: International Organization for Standardization, an international standard-setting body composed of representatives from various national standards organizations.
- LAN: Local-area network.
- LAPB: Link Access Protocol, Balanced, a serial protocol.

- Layer 2: Layer 2 of the OSI model, also called data link. In the Data Center the dominant Layer 2 protocol is Ethernet.
- Layer 2 Multipath: An alternative to spanning tree to increase Layer 2 bandwidth.
- Layer 3: Layer 3 of the OSI model, also called internetworking. The dominant Layer 3 protocol is IP, both IPv4 and IPv6.
- Layer 4: Layer 4 of the OSI model, also called transport. The dominant Layer 4 protocol is TCP.
- Layer 7: Layer 7 of the OSI model, also called application. It contains all applications that use the network.
- LLC: Logical Link Control, a key protocol in IEEE 802.1.
- LLC2: LLC used with reliable delivery.
- LLDP: Link Layer Discovery Protocol, an Ethernet configuration protocol, also known as IEEE 802.1AB.
- Lossless network: A network that does not lose frames under congestion.
- Lossy network: A network that loses frames under congestion.
- MPI: Message Passing Interface, an IPC API.
- N_Port: A Fibre Channel port that connects to an F_Port.
- N_Port_ID: Fibre Channel address, aka FC_ID.
- NFS: Network File System.
- NIC: Network Interface Card.
- Node: A host or storage array in Fibre Channel.
- OSI: Open Systems Interconnection.
- OUI: Organization Unique Identifiers – a 24 bits prefix.
- PAUSE: A frame that causes the transmission on an Ethernet link to pause for a specified amount of time.
- PCI: Peripheral Component Interconnect, a standard I/O bus.
- PFC: Priority-based Flow Control, aka PPP.
- PPP: Per Priority Pause, aka PFC.
- QCN: Quantized Congestion Notification, a congestion management algorithm.
- RAM: Random Access Memory
- R_RDY: Receiver Ready, an ordered set used in Fibre Channel to replenish buffer-to-buffer credits.
- RDMA: Remote Direct Memory Access, an IPC technique.
- RDS: Reliable Datagram Service, an IPC interface used by databases.
- RED: Random Early Detect, an AQM technique.

- RSCN: Registered State Change Notification, an event notification protocol in Fibre Channel.
- SAN: Storage Area Network.
- SCSI: Small Computer System Interface.
- SDP: Socket Direct Protocol, an IPC interface that mimics TCP sockets.
- SFP+: Small Form-Factor Pluggable transceiver.
- SPMA: Server Provided MAC Address.
- STP: Spanning Tree Protocol, see also IEEE 802.1Q.
- T11: Technical Committee 11, the committee responsible for Fibre Channel (www.t11.org).
- TCAM: Ternary Context Addressable Memory.
- TCP: Transmission Control Protocol, a transport layer protocol in IP.
- TOE: TCP Offload Engine.
- TRILL: Transparent Interconnection of Lots of Links, Working Group within the IETF.
- Twinax: A twin micro-coaxial copper cable used for 10GE.
- VE_Port: An FCoE port on an FCoE switch used to interconnect another FCoE switch.
- VF_Port: An FCoE port on an FCoE switch used to interconnect an ENode.
- VLAN: Virtual LAN.
- VN_Port: An FCoE port on an ENode used to interconnect an FCoE switch.
- Wireshark: A public domain protocol analyzer (http://www.wireshark.org/).
- Zoning: An access control mechanism in Fibre Channel fabrics.

Figures

Tables

Index

Symbols

10GBASE-T, 7, 141
10GE, 5, 6, 7, 9, 28, 38, 65–66, 127–130, 132, 141
802.1, 20, 22, 28, 46, 51, 54, 61, 66, 139, 141–142
802.1Q, 9, 20, 23, 51, 81, 141, 143, 145
802.1Qau, 25
802.1Qaz, 22–23
802.1Qbb, 20
802.3, 8, 16, 20, 139, 141
802.3ad, 32

A

Access Control Lists, 9, 103
Active Queue Management, 8, 19, 141
Additive Increase, Multiplicative Decrease, 26
Advertisement, 98, 100–102, 108–109
API, 13
ARP, 9, 45

B

B2B, 8, 11, 141
Backward Congestion Notification, 25, 141
Blade Servers, 2, 131–133, 137
Buffer, 8–9, 11–12, 17–19, 26, 64
Buffer-to-Buffer, 8, 16–17, 141

C

CAM, 9
Catalyst, 34, 126, 135
Cluster, 4
CNA, 2–3, 6, 82, 84, 87, 99, 108, 110–113, 126, 129, 141
Collisions, 16
Congestion Management, 22–23, 25, 141
Congestion, 26
Converged Enhanced Ethernet, 66, 141
Converged Network Adapter, 2, 74, 87, 110, 141

CRC, 16, 80–81, 141
Credits, 8, 16–18
Cut-through, 9–10

D

Data Center, 1–2, 4, 6–9, 11, 16–17, 22, 28, 38, 40, 42, 50, 61–64, 66–67, 84, 111, 119, 121, 125–127, 129, 137, 141–142
Data Center Bridging, 22, 66, 120, 141
Data Center Ethernet, 66, 141
DCBX, 19, 22–23, 66–67, 141
Deadlock, 8, 19
Deficit Weighted Round Robin, 23, 141
D_ID, 76, 86–87
Discovery Advertisement, 75, 77, 96
Discovery Protocol, 22, 75–77, 97–98, 102, 142
DMA, 10
Domain ID, 86–87
DWRR, 23, 141

E

Enhanced Transmission Selection, 23
ENode, 74–77, 82, 91–92, 97–104, 108–110, 141
E_Port, 84
Errors, 8, 11–12, 16
Etherchannel, 32–34, 50–51, 59, 90, 128–129, 133
Ethernet, 1, 3–6, 8–11, 13, 15–16, 19, 25–26, 66, 82, 84–90, 103, 106, 111, 119, 125–129, 131–134, 141–142
Ethernet Host Virtualizer, 36, 127–128, 137
Ethernet Link Aggregation, 90
ETS, 22–23

F

Fabric Provided MAC Addresses, 90, 142
Fast Ethernet, 16
FC-BB-5, 67, 84, 91, 108, 119, 121, 141
FC-CRC, 70

CISCO.

I/O Consolidation in the Data Center

A complete guide to Data Center Ethernet and Fibre Channel over Ethernet

Silvano Gai
Claudio DeSanti

ciscopress.com

FREE Online Edition

Your purchase of **I/O Consolidation in the Data Center** includes access to a free online edition for 45 days through the Safari Books Online subscription service. Nearly every Cisco Press book is available online through Safari Books Online, along with more than 5,000 other technical books and videos from publishers such as Addison-Wesley Professional, Exam Cram, IBM Press, O'Reilly, Prentice Hall, Que, and Sams.

SAFARI BOOKS ONLINE allows you to search for a specific answer, cut and paste code, download chapters, and stay current with emerging technologies.

Activate your FREE Online Edition at www.informit.com/safarifree

> **STEP 1:** Enter the coupon code: KEBUPVH.

> **STEP 2:** New Safari users, complete the brief registration form.
> Safari subscribers, just log in.

If you have difficulty registering on Safari or accessing the online edition, please e-mail customer-service@safaribooksonline.com

Safari
Books Online

Addison Wesley · Adobe Press · ALPHA · Cisco Press · FT Press · IBM Press · lynda.com · Microsoft Press · New Riders

O'REILLY · Peachpit Press · PRENTICE HALL · Que · Redbooks · SAMS · SAS Publishing · Sun Microsystems · WILEY